FAMILY HOME

Screaming

FAMILY HOME

creaming

Robert Kirby and Pat Bagley

SLICKROCK
BOOKS

ISBN 1-892936-08-9

10 9 8 7 6 5 4 3 2 1

DEDICATION

This book is dedicated to the average
American parents and their 1.7 kids,
even though it's really against the law
to cut kids in half like that.

FOREWORD

In 1997, the editor of the *Salt Lake Tribune* loosed me on humanity in general. My weekly column, which heretofore had lampooned primarily Mormons every Saturday, was upgraded to include the rest of the world on Tuesday and Thursday.

This was good and bad. Good because it significantly increased the number of targets for my chosen career of mindless heckling. Bad because the new target-rich environment included close friends and family, or, in other words, the weirdest people I know.

Everything you read here about my family and friends is true. Furthermore, I have not changed their names to protect their identities. It's my way of getting even. However, some clarification is necessary.

My wife, Irene, is actually a nice person. Making her sound like a dark overlordess is simply my way of making a generally overlooked point about the magic and wonder of marriage.

Namely that real men fear their wives.

It's my kids who are evil. I've raised (mostly) three daughters: Christie, Autumn and Ginny. Actually, my wife raised them. Beyond continuing to hold a job and staying out of jail, I had no idea what to do once conception had been achieved. For me, fatherhood amounts to little more than self defense.

This explains why, even though I participated in their lives, today I still have no idea what makes my daughters tick. I comfort myself with the thought that neither does God.

Finally, like most guys, I seem to have a lot of exceptionally stupid friends. Most of the trouble I've seen involved at least one or two of them. When it comes to having an interesting life, you can't beat stupid friends. That's your wife's job.

Robert Kirby
Springville, Utah
July 21, 1999

TRACTOR WOMEN

I used to be a kid. I could prove it to you with carbon dating, but that's expensive. You'll have to take my word for it.

When I was a kid, one of the things my dad did that drove me crazy was to compare his childhood with mine. He was always on me about how unfair life had been to him at my age.

If Dad came home and found me talking on the phone with my girlfriend instead of mowing the lawn, he pointed out how good I had it.

"During the Depression, we never talked on phones. We cut grass with clippers until our fingers bled. We were lucky if bears and Indians didn't—"

"You didn't have phones back then, Dad."

"We did too, smart-aleck. There was one down at the Ivy Market. What we never had was long hair like that. When I was a kid, boys were boys and girls..."

I made a promise to myself that I would never do this sort of thing to my own kids. After all, who was I to insist that my children relive my life?

Once she got to know me—or, more specifically, what I had been like as a kid—my wife agreed. This was, she said, a promise that I should keep if I knew what was good for me. No way did she want me grouching about not having the time to do homework when I was a kid because I was too busy sitting in detention.

Over the years, I've kept silent on the subject of what I call "generational fairness." Until now.

The straw that broke the camel's back, neck and pelvis was the back-to-school clothing safari that my wife and daughters undertook last Saturday. I don't mind them shopping for clothes. After all, the one thing a father wants —especially if he remembers anything at all about when he was a kid—is his daughters wearing clothes. Lots and lots of clothes.

What gets me is the clothes themselves. Namely the styles.

What is it with girls today that they want to look like Tractor Women? Boots, overalls and cropped hair. Not only is it unattractive, it costs more than a brain hemorrhage.

When I was a kid, a tie-dyed t-shirt, jeans and some sneakers did it for us. Sure, we looked stupid, but it only cost us ten bucks. Fifteen if we accessorized with a string of beads, a bandanna and a peace sign button.

My haircut cost...wait a minute. I didn't get one from 1968–70. Never mind.

Today, it's 160 bucks for fashionable L'il Abner boots, fifty bucks for designer overalls and forty for a haircut that would embarrass a Dublin street urchin. Did someone see Cindy Crawford dressed up to plow the north 40 and mistake it for a fashion statement?

Somewhere along the way, looking like you were raised in an abandoned grain silo started costing a lot of money.

While such things are traditionally worse for girls, the guys aren't much better off. Why does it take seventeen yards of denim to make a single pair of pants? A kid walked past my house yesterday wearing a pair of giant pants. It looked like two pup tents having a race.

Furthermore, letting said pants hang in such a way that it advertises your butt should really be the province of people who actually have butts. Am I right?

Maybe all these baggy clothes are a political statement. My own teenage dress code certainly was. It said that we were against the Establishment, the Vietnam War and "Leave it to Beaver." What does dressing like a gangsta say, "I'm unemployed and underprivileged, so please do a drive-by on me?"

Ironically, there is one thing that hasn't changed from my generation to this one. Namely the people who foot the bill for this nonsense. Mom and Dad. They're the ones who pay for it. So, if anyone has a right to complain...

THE WAY
WE WEREN'T

When I was 15, I came across my father's high school year-books. It wasn't like he was trying to hide them or any-thing. In fact, he was proud that he'd been president of his senior class. I remember thinking, "So what?" In 1949 Whackhead, Idaho, that's got to be the equivalent of being named prom queen at a school for the blind.

Looking at my father's high school year book brought me to a disturbing conclusion, namely that he'd gone to high school with an uncommon number of Martians. I'm serious. The entire class of 1948 was a collection of slick-haired, cross-eyed, buck-toothed goofs.

"Ha!" I said to my dad. "Look at the hair styles on these trolls."

My comments didn't hurt my dad's feelings as much as they hurt my head. Dad took the book away, whacked me with it, and stuck it back in the trunk.

"Some day," he said, "your kids will think the same thing about your high school pictures."

Never happen, I thought. At the time it was 1969 and everyone in the world was wearing floppy bell bottom pants, paisley shirts, head bands and wild hair. Tie-dyed clothing was groovy and platform shoes were far out. It was the age of Aquarius and we were all flower children and outasight.

I wish we were still out of sight. Time warped on me last week when my daughters found my yearbooks and pictures. They nearly went into convulsions laughing at the groovy class of 1971.

"Nice hair, Dad," one daughter said. "It's frizzed clear out to your shoulders. It looks like you got hit by lightning."

"Oh my gosh," another daughter cried. "Look at his clown shoes."

"Did your girlfriend iron her hair to make it that straight? She looks like Morticia Addams."

There was no telling my daughters that styles change from generation to generation, and that my grandkids would soon be making fun of them. Like every generation before them, they think cool is a constant that began with them.

In a few years, these little twerps with their spaceman hair cuts are going to be hiding pictures of themselves from their own kids. My son-in-law has a haircut that would get him executed in some Communist countries. He doesn't know it yet. In fact, he probably won't know it until 15 years from now when his kids find his yearbook and tell him that his head looks like a road-kill porcupine.

The saddest parts about stupid styles are the people who can't give them up. I still see guys my age trapped in the Age of Aquarius. They're still walking around dressed in Dead Head gear. Or women in their fifties who haven't clued in to the fact that hair lacquered and styled into something resembling the horns on a water buffalo has long been out of style.

Some styles come full swing. Long hair for guys, which has never gone completely out of style, has been largely replaced by short hair, or shaved heads into which rats have nibbled intricate designs.

For girls, mini skirts were the rage when I was young. There were replaced by granny skirts in the 70s. We've come back now to mini skirts, which may or may not be in answer to one of my prayers. I hope I'm dead before granny skirts reappear.

One thing remains the same from generation to generation. Being oblivious to ridiculousness has always been the price of cool. The bill for it just doesn't come due for fifteen or twenty years.

SEXUAL MORASSMENT

You may as well charge me with it right now. There was a time in my life when I sexually harassed women. I'm not proud of it. My only defense is that it occurred when I was in the second grade.

Apparently that's no longer an adequate defense. Thirty years later, I could still get sued for what happened on the monkey bars at Garfield Elementary School.

I decided to go public with this dark secret after hearing about Johnathan Prevette, a 6-year-old Lexington, North Carolina boy suspended from his elementary school last month for allegedly kissing a female classmate.

However, when authorities discovered that Prevette's victim asked him to kiss her, they let him out on a $100,000 bond, or something like that.

Truth is, Prevette got off light. He should have been expelled for good and branded a social menace. I mean what kind of a world do we live in where heinous behavior like that warrants a mere slap on the wrist? Hasn't Prevette ever heard of cooties? Sheesh.

The first woman I ever sexually harassed was Sandy McFarland, a buck-toothed seven-year-old screecher with hair the color of a traffic flare. When I accidentally bumped up against her while playing tether ball, by best friend Leon bellowed, "Kirby's got Sandy's cooties!"

Could there have been anything worse? I didn't know whether to wet my pants or kill myself. No matter how hard I tried to pass Sandy's cooties on to some other unfortunate, I couldn't. All the guys threw rocks or ran away from me.

I had to do something to regain my social standing. I accomplished this by looking up Sandy's dress when she climbed the monkey bars. Then I told everyone what color her underpants were. After school, Sandy hit me so hard it took two teachers to find my glasses. Take it from me, cooties with a knuckle chaser are the worst kind, man.

I also sexually harassed Pansy "Moose Lips" Penninger by stealing her Minnie Mouse lunch box and not giving it back until she tackled Leon and kissed him three times on the face.

Poor Leon never got over this disgrace. The last I heard, it took him two tries before he made it to the third grade. He's probably still going through rehab somewhere.

My worst sexual harassment offense occurred in fourth grade when I sat behind Tina Mae Briedenbach in band. One day, she turned around and accused me of blowing spit on her from my trombone. When she giggled and stuck her tongue out, something tore loose in my heart.

After that, all I could do was stare at Tina Mae's dark hair and chase her unmercifully during recess. The hell with safe sex, I wanted those cooties. When she deliberately gave them to Kevin Freehouse, life wasn't worth living. My mom had to ground me to keep me from laying in the road.

Things got better in fifth grade when Tina Mae kissed me on the lips for half of my moon pie and eight cents. To this day, I can't pass moon pies in the grocery store without feeling young again.

Like Prevette, somebody should have done something about me back then. I wouldn't have gone on to high school addicted to cooties so bad that I actually took girls on dates.

Eventually, I even harassed a woman right into marrying me. Twenty years later, I still want her cooties. Am I sick or what?

There it is, my awful past. If Prevette and I ever get nominated to the Supreme Court, we wouldn't last five minutes in a Senate hearing. Sandy would show up and tell everyone about the monkey bars. Times being what they are, I'd be lucky not to get lynched.

My victims probably all grew up and became radical and bulimic feminist lesbians. There's not much I can do about that now. All I can do is apologize. Sandy, Pansy and Tina Mae, wherever you are, I'm sorry. But thanks for the cooties.

H O M E ALONE MOAN

There was a time when the bachelor life suited me. This isn't it. Last week, my wife went to Canada to visit her mother. She's only been gone for a few days and I already hate being single again.

We actually looked forward to the time apart. While she packed, Irene and I joked about me "baching it." For me, that meant total freedom. For Irene, it meant that I'd live on cold cereal, take my underwear off with a steam cleaner and come down with dysentery and ringworm.

Except for three weeks I spent at Ft. Benning in 1976, this is the longest stretch that we've been separated. We thought it would be interesting to see how much we missed each other again.

I never told Irene that I didn't miss her one bit when I went to Ft. Benning. Someone there was always berating me for being a lazy, ignorant slob. Except for the push-ups and getting thrown out of an airplane at the end of the three weeks, it felt exactly like home.

I didn't plan on missing Irene this time, either. As soon as she drove away, I called up Larry to see if he wanted to get rowdy. He couldn't come over because, unlike me, his wife was still in town.

So instead, I watered the lawn, weeded the garden, did two loads of laundry, walked the dog, ran some errands, made dinner and cleaned out the storage shed.

At midnight, I collapsed and dragged myself to bed alone because I had to go to work in the morning. Incidentally, this was the only time that I felt like a bachelor during the last week.

Bachelor life used to be more simple than this. Twenty years ago, I lived in my car and out of my pockets. When I cashed my pay check, I put some gas in the car and a little something toward outstanding traffic fines. The rest went into my pocket where I squandered it, ending up broke a week before I got paid again.

Somewhere between then and now, being a bachelor has become more complicated. For example, I used to be able to do my laundry by just spraying a can of Right Guard on it. Now, I have to add bleach, fabric softener and stain remover.

The stuff I ate as a bachelor now paralyzes my digestion. Three days ago, I ate an entire combination pizza. It's still in there causing me trouble. I'd eat some prunes but then I'd have to stay close to the bathroom. I'm not as quick or as nimble as I used to be.

I don't tolerate mess and clutter like I once did. I once moved a pile of dirty clothes and motorcycle parts in my bachelor apartment and found a bus stop bench that Bush Man had stolen three months before. And this was after the cops searched the place twice looking for the bench and hadn't found it.

Today, I can't sleep if I leave my socks on the floor. Too many years with Irene has irrevocably altered my mess thermostat. I find myself laying in bed at night, fretting over the poor job our self-cleaning oven is doing.

One thing hasn't changed: I'm still a lecher. The difference being that when I was a bachelor, I had standards even if they weren't very high. I also could (and frequently did) go for months between romantic interludes.

Now, after twenty years of semi-regular loving, I go through withdrawals when Irene leaves for just a few days. Women I previously found only marginally attractive begin to look like Vogue models. Yesterday, I saw a gorgeous brunette sashaying past the house. It wasn't until I rubbed my eyes that I realized it was the neighbor's spaniel.

I've got another five days to go. Then, Irene will come home and I can go back to being a happy-go-lucky married guy.

CRUEL
AND USUAL

Greg and I once dragged a friend of ours a mile after he fell while water skiing. When we realized that Larry wouldn't or couldn't let go of the rope, we had some fun. We were careful not to kill him because, frankly, that can be expensive.

When we got him back in the boat, Larry retched up ten gallons of water and a salamander. Then he had the audacity to impugn our friendship by demanding to know why we did not stop sooner.

"You didn't give the proper hand signal," I said. "Besides, after we dragged you out of your suit, Greg laughed so hard that he passed out. Now we can shave his head."

I feel sorry for women. It takes a guy to really know what friends are for.

This sad biological fact underscores one of the primary differences between men and women—something that no amount of feminist folderol or sensitivity training will ever fix. Guys get off on the pain and emotional suffering of other guys, especially if said other guys are their friends.

It's true. If a woman sees another woman with a tiny smudge on her blouse—even if the other woman was a complete stranger and better looking—she would immediately tell the woman so as

to prevent her from suffering embarrassment.

First Woman: "Pardon me, but you have a tiny bit of gua-camole on your sleeve. I thought you might want to know."

Second Woman: "Oh, my goodness! Thank you so much. By the way, who does your hair? It's wonderful."

Can you see your average guy doing this? And by this I mean guys who are not ecclesiastical leaders or somehow involved in EST training. Normal guys actually go out of their way to embarrass each other.

Guy 1: "OK, nobody tell Bill that he's got seagull poop on his head."

Guy 2: "This is so cool. And on his wedding day, too."

It doesn't have to be something accidental either. Guys deliberately say mean things to each other in the hopes that there will be a laugh in it. The better the friendship, the worse the insult. My best friend Greg and I are so close that we have actually driven each other into therapy.

Women, being the natural peacemakers (and liars) that they

are, will do anything to avoid saying or doing something to another woman's face that will make her feel bad.

Woman #1: "Have you been losing weight? You look so trim."

Woman #2: "Thank you. I've been working out. And how about you? Is that a new blouse?"

There is something in a Y chromosome that prevents males from sparing the feelings of other males.

Guy 1: "Ralph, that butt of yours belongs on a Saudi oil tanker. Have you been eating lard straight from the can again?"

Guy 2: "Speaking of butts, isn't that one poking out of your collar?"

If women said stuff like this to each other, they would never be able to leave the house again. For guys, these are bonding words.

It's the same thing with personal safety. Women will apologize if they so much as bump into each other. If they accidentally trip each other, the apology lasts for days. They bring each other treats and animal figurines.

Not guys. When Greg and I visited the Grand Canyon last year, neither of us would go near the edge while the other was anywhere close. Ditto the campground outhouses, which are prime bonding traps, especially when roped shut and set on fire.

I wouldn't mention any of this except that I am going to visit Greg next week. If I am not back in a week, it means we are still very close. Please call the police and my primary care physician.

PALS
OR GALS

had lots of friends when I got married. Actually, they were pals. Friends are people who share your interests and make you feel good about yourself. They help you achieve your goals and defend you against your enemies.

Pals are more than friends. Pals put you in touch with stuff most people will never experience. Like jail. Pals also keep you from reaching your goals, and they help you collect enemies. As such, pals tend to be more fun than friends.

Before getting married, my closest pals and I fished, hunted, partied and plotted the downfall of civilization together. Nothing, including the draft board and the police, could tear us apart. Or so we thought. One by one, we all got married.

One of life's biggest rules is that a guy can no longer be pals once he gets married. Certainly not if he plans on staying married. It's not that you don't want to still be pals, but rather that you no longer have any say. Women have all the say. A sensible woman does not want her husband to stay close with his pre-marital pals. She knows that her husband's pals represent the call of the wild. The problem rests in the way the two genders view marriage. For women, the whole marital bliss plan is simple.

1. Find potential husband.
2. Marry him.
3. Cut him off from pals.
4. Civilize him.

Men never see this coming. We think that when we marry a woman, she will be a softer version of a pal. As such, a woman should fit right into our version of marriage, which is:

1. Attract woman by being a bum.
2. Marry woman.
3. Continue being a bum.

A guy's first clue that his plan is doomed is when his wife sweetly says something to the effect that she does not want to spend her honeymoon in a fish camp. Then she won't let the dog into bed. Later, she introduces stuff like cutlery, soap and a budget.

Additional warning signs are feminine utterances like "No, you are not going to use my Tupperware money to bail Rusty out of jail" and "I don't want Ed sleeping in our garage anymore."

A woman further alienates her husband from his pals by making him do traditionally non-guy stuff. Things like going to church, doing dishes, wearing underwear and taking her on dates seven years after they are married, and therefore technically a waste of money.

She also gradually makes her husband's pals feel unwanted. It starts out simple, like telling her husband's pals that he cannot go fishing for a whole month because he has to earn a living. She also fits words like "responsibility," "maturity" and "personal hygiene" into the conversation whenever possible.

If the pal still fails to get the hint, the woman becomes slightly less subtle and starts calling the police whenever said pal drops by.

The most troubling part is that there really is no way a guy can hang on to his pals. Eventually they get married, too. And if you think your wife's eyes narrow when your friends show up, wait until you see the looks their wives start giving you.

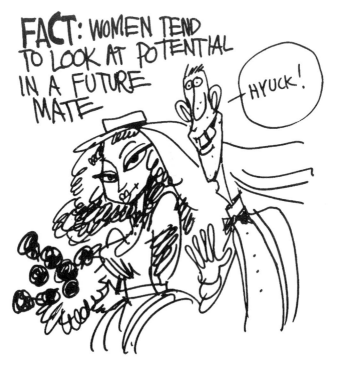

"No, Bill cannot go rat hunting at the dump. We have Lamaze class tonight. In fact, we have it every night for the next eleven years. Or until we move."

Gradually, you lose touch with your pals. Since caller ID came into being, I haven't been able to get any of my former pals on the phone. Oddly enough, they have also stopped calling me.

The sooner a guy faces up to the fact that he can't be a pal anymore, the sooner he will come around to the realization that he is happily married.

UP CHICK CRICK

just got back from vacation. My family spent a week camping near Mesa Verde National Park. Not real camping. More like chick camping.

Forget equal rights, there are only two kinds of camping: Guy camping and chick camping. And don't let anyone fool you, guy camping is tough. Chick camping, however, is a nightmare.

I didn't know this of course. I've been out of the camping loop for a while. But when I did camp, I guy camped. I didn't take 400 pounds of bathroom gear and fuzzy bunny slippers into the woods. And I didn't whine because the bathroom had a spider in it. If a park ranger was rude to me, I considered myself lucky that he at least didn't shoot at me.

As a kid, I was a camping fool. I could spend two weeks in the woods with nothing but a hammer and a bag of Oreos. I left my underwear at home with my morality. Any camping trip was a complete loss if my mother didn't throw up or call the police when she saw me coming up the driveway.

Because the women in our family (including the damn dogs)

outnumber me five to one, we chick camped this year. Here's what we did: We loaded two-thirds of everything we owned into a camp trailer and then burned the guts out of our Jeep dragging it to Colorado.

In the long run, it probably would have been cheaper to jack up our house and take it with us. We would still have forgotten something, though. An important part of chick camping is forgetting stuff. Then you can stop in every town and buy what you forgot: bug spray, deodorant, hand lotion, lip gloss, a new hair style, love seat, etc.

The most arduous part of chick camping is choosing the campsite. In guy camping, this is the easy part. Guys camp precisely where we collapse from exhaustion and animal bites. Particular we ain't. Guy campsites could double as grave sites.

Location is very important in chick camping. It's a holdover from the pioneer days when women made men camp next to water for culinary purposes. Nowadays, women still make men camp next to water. It's called a restroom.

Pulling into our campground—which turned out to be exactly like our house only with a dirt floor, trees and a more crowded bathroom—we spent an hour jockeying for a spot.

"Now this place is okay, honey, but there's just a bit too much sun, we aren't close enough to the pool and you can't even see the game room from here. Oh no, look, there are 25 camp trailers here just like ours."

In guy camping, you call it crowded if there are campers in the same time zone as you. At Mesa Verde, two guys I thought were French—but turned out to be from San Francisco—camped on one side of us. They could have given us chick camping lessons. Worse, a family of loud rubes who cooked Spaghetti-O's every night camped on the other side.

Once, on a particularly memorable guy camp in Washington, I watched a bear eat all our food, a shark eat one of our kayaks and a raccoon whiz on a sleeping bag. At Mesa Verde, my daughters panicked when a moth flew into the tent trailer.

Cost is another thing. Chick camping is expensive because chick camping includes shopping and going on rides. When you chick camp, you always come home with more than you took. Guy campers, on the other hand, are lucky to come home alive. Guy camping is expensive only if you include the medical bills and court fines.

But I'm being unfair. There's a plus to chick camping. It's relaxing. This year was the first time my annual vacation wasn't immediately followed by extended sick leave.

EXORCISE YOUR THIGHS

My wife bought a Health Rider from some sales guy who saw her coming from the other side of the moon. It's the latest in fitness gimmicks that have passed through and out of our lives. We've alternately tried a stationary bike, something-or-other invented by a psychotic Apache and a jogging trampoline.

At first, I wasn't impressed with the Health Rider. Viewed from a distance, it looks like someone trying to row a starved horse. I laughed when I first saw it. And it's a good thing I was at a distance because my wife was doing the rowing.

"That's not exercise," I said. "It's entertainment."

My wife eventually got me on the Health Rider the same way women have always gotten men to do things they didn't want to do: ridicule our masculinity. She sniped at me until I tried it.

"See?" I said, cranking away like a galley slave. "It doesn't do anything for you. It's too easy." Fifteen seconds later, I coughed up my heart.

I used to be in better shape. In fact, there was a time when I was in terrific shape. At 19, I could chug 10 miles through a

Georgia forest in August carrying a pack and an M-60 machine-gun, and the only real hardship was that the drill sergeant wouldn't let me smoke while I ran.

That was then, this is now. Today, I'm lucky if I can climb a flight of stairs without losing the feeling in my hands and feet. The most exercise I get in a day is thinking about looking for the television remote control.

Anyway, I've started riding Ol' Blue every morning. It's pure agony, in part because Blue hates me. In addition to making me sore enough to shriek hysterically for a medic, he's also thrown me twice. But he's better than some of the other fitness gizmos I've tried, a few of which should be outlawed by OSHA if not Mother Nature.

The jogging trampoline was a complete waste. Boing, boing, boing, boing. Where's the point? The only weight I ever lost came from bleeding after I boinged too hard and got whacked in the head by the ceiling fan.

The stationary bike just wasn't me either. Ever since my mission, riding hard on a bike seems kind of pointless unless you're being chased by a pack of ravenous village dogs.

I've tried but never actually owned a Nordic Track. It might be because I'm not coordinated enough to keep my arms and legs and brain moving in harmony. Or it might be that I just don't see the attraction in pretending that I'm skiing in my family room.

Still, I have to do a lot of pretending on Ol' Blue. It's the only way I can make myself do it. The reality of 43-year-old man wheezing away on something that isn't a horse, a bike a rowboat would be more than I could bear otherwise.

My favorite exercise fantasy is that I'm a Pony Express rider trying to outrun some Indians. The other day I thought I'd caught an arrow in the back but it turned out that one of my vertebrae had just popped out onto the floor.

Sometimes I pretend that I'm crewing for Harvard and we're in a big race with Yale. This fantasy is a little harder to maintain because the truth is that I wouldn't give a rat's ass if either school burned down.

All of this naturally brings us to the reason why men put themselves through the agony of exercise. It's the same reason that originally brought us out of the forest and encouraged us to eat with forks. The exact same thing that made us go out and invent stuff like fire, automatic transmissions and aftershave. Women.

A very important study that I forget the name of indicated that most men exercise because they want to appear buff for women. When women look at a guy, he wants them to see Alec Baldwin, not John Candy. He also wants them to blush with passion for him, forgetting every time that women never do stuff like that unless they're really drunk.

The really crazy thing here is that women exercise for the exact same reason men do: women. I'm serious. Women wear makeup and expensive clothing for the same reason they spend two hours on their hair in order to go to the store for five minutes. So that other women won't talk about them behind their backs.

Whatever the reason, suffice it to say that exercise is good for you, unless, of course, it results in death. If that happens, fitness experts generally agree that it's not as good for you. It's also important to avoid debilitating injuries such as hamstring pulls, shin splints, hernias, hemorrhoids, and large dog bites. Stuff like this tends to detract from the point of exercise, namely that you'll be more healthy.

The most effective exercise machine I've ever used was a drill sergeant. Not some lizard-thin gal in Spandex chirping, "C'mon! Uh-huh!" either. I mean a real military drill sergeant bellowing insults about my mother while slamming his fist on my helmet. You don't have to supply your own motivation in a case like this. The Army issues it to you.

It's been my experience that a real fitness program shouldn't just hurt. It should scar you for life. Shoot, I'll bet I could lose five pounds right now if a furious neanderthal in a Smokey the Bear hat merely glanced in my direction.

VITAL VICTUALS

Approximately twice a month my wife and I go grocery shopping. We've long believed that selecting and purchasing a balanced diet for our family requires input from both of us. One person to choose the family's nutritional needs and the other to sack it up and lug it out to the car.

As a witless beast of burden, my sole grocery shopping responsibility is to push a grocery cart. The first proof that grocery shopping is the sole province of women is right here with these carts.

All grocery carts drive like they've been driven *and* maintained by women. This explains why even though I choose carefully, I always get a cart with wheels so far out of alignment that it drives like someone ran it from one end of Baja to the other at 200 mph.

Seriously, no man worthy of his testosterone really likes to grocery shop. Any man who does was probably a cheerleader in high school. Maybe it's because as a gender, it's hard for men to

get past the shame of bringing home food that we didn't actually kill or steal ourselves.

Women are cool with choosing food from a shelf. They know all that grams and percentage stuff listed on the package. The only thing men know instinctively about buying food is how many bites per package. For Hostess products it's usually one. For roasts, canned hams and whole turkeys, it can be as many as five or six.

No man, even if he's a professor of mathematics, knows how to figure out the pound to price ratio, something that women come by as naturally as ovulation. My wife can tell with a single glance if something is a good buy. If it's the right time of month, she can peg it down to a tenth of a cent including the gas it took to drive to the store to buy it.

Nutrition is something men and women differ greatly on as well. A balanced meal for women consists of selections from all the food groups. For women, there are hundreds of food groups, some of which consist of things that I wouldn't want on the bottom of my shoe much lessen my plate.

Men only have two food groups: food that's yummy and food that's not. A typical balanced meal for a guy is jerky, corn chips, four Milky Way bars and something fizzy to wash it all down. If there's no soda pop, we'll stir some sugar into a glass of Alka-Seltzer. Hey, you gotta have fizz to grow up big and strong.

Women typically like food that's green—lettuce, string beans, spinach, zucchini. For men, that's not food, that's what food eats. Also, green is an indication that the food it dangerous. We learned long ago not to eat green meat no matter how hungry we were because it could kill us. Why take chances now?

Maybe it's because women actually prepare most of the food that makes them the best at buying it. They go to the store with a menu whereas men go to the store with a wallet and about four brain cells.

When my wife goes to the store for dinner, she comes home with the fixings for porkchops, salad and rice pilaf. When I go, I return with a two quarts of motor oil, pork rinds, a "TV Guide" and a nagging feeling that I've forgotten something more or less important.

Despite significant strides in the area of domestic equal rights, men still aren't allowed to fix food for children. In our house this is because I once fixed our children malt ball and Frito soup for lunch. I came close to being the first Beat dead Dad.

All I'm really good for is lugging the groceries out to the car. That and eating most of them.

PIECES
ON EARTH

If you are reading this and have not yet purchased the exact Christmas gift your wife wanted, we have less than 24 hours to save your life.

Calm down. I have lots of experience with this. Though married for 23 years, I have never gotten my wife exactly what she wanted for Christmas. That's because I have always been dumb enough to take her at her word.

When asked what they want for Christmas, most women invariably ask for one of two things. It's either "Oh, just whatever, dear" or "Harrison Ford." The first, of course, is a lie. "Whatever" really means something specific and you better have been paying attention when they started hinting about it back in April.

I can't help you with the second.

"Whatever" is pretty dumb considering how long you've been married to your particular spouse. Whether it's five or 25 years, most women will not come right out and say what men need to hear, namely, "Get me that particular thing there in blue no matter how much it costs, or you're dead."

However, just because you think you know what to buy doesn't mean you're off dangerous ground. You still have to pay for it. And according to national statistics, this is easy for only half of all marriages—the half that manages the money. Which, if you have a lot of facial hair, is probably not you.

It's the big Christmas adult mystery: How does the spouse who doesn't handle the family finances buy something for the spouse that does? By special mandate from the utility companies and the bank, my wife manages our finances.

I don't even know how much money we have. It could be five bucks or $5 million. Irene could buy the Utah Jazz for me and I wouldn't know it until Christmas morning when I found John Stockton under my tree with a bow stuck on his head.

On the other hand, all my wife has to do is look in the checkbook to know what I got her for Christmas. If I wrote a check for $189.99 plus tax to Kountry Kitsch, she knows I got her that Three Stooges bread mixer she liked. She says she doesn't look, but every holiday season she's bugging me, "You better hurry up if you're going to get me anything for Christmas."

I've tried being sneaky, just drawing the money out of our joint account so there's no paper trail. Doesn't work. My wife sees that the money is gone and grills me like I took it for a secret trip to Wendover or something. Never mind that it's Christmas and there just *might* be a legitimate reason for it.

Finally, unless it's something small like jewels, gold or an IOU, spouses tend to get each other large gifts like dishwashers, televisions, or new cars. The size alone makes it tough to hide them before Christmas.

I once hid a gift to my wife at the neighbor's. Unfortunately, his wife thought it was for her and pretended not to notice so as not to spoil the "surprise" on Christmas morning. Guess who got surprised when she didn't get a new oak chest of drawers. Sheesh, we could hear the sound of them fighting clear over at our house.

Be careful when you're on Christmas Dangerous Ground. You could end up giving and getting more than you bargained for on Christmas morning.

U N H A N D Y - MAN

I thought I might save a little money this year and drive myself nuts instead of paying someone else to do it for me. Either way it costs a lot of money.

It's easy. All I have to do is listen to my wife when she tells me to start fixing things around the house. Like most urban males, I can shave 30 points off an already dubious IQ by simply picking up a pair of pliers.

This situation makes it tough to decide if I want to spend more money than I currently have to fix those things myself, or more money than I will ever have in my entire life to have a professional do it.

Or I could just shoot myself.

It's not that I mind doing mechanically complicated chores. It's that I suffer from a serious malady common to males of my generation: "fixus stupidus." It means that although I earn a living as a writer, I can't decipher simple written instructions. My parents discovered this when they gave me a set of Tinker Toys one Christmas and I couldn't figure out how to use them. I thought they were poorly designed pencils and erasers.

"He's 22 years old, for crying out loud," my dad said to my mom. "It's your fault. I told you we should have gone with a dachshund."

Over the years, I got better at fixing things. I fixed the bathroom the last time it broke. You have to go outside and turn on the water in the backyard to flush the toilet, but technically it works.

I also fixed the refrigerator light by installing an aircraft landing light that stayed on even when the door was closed. We're the only family on the whole block that can bake a ham in their Frigidaire. My daughters use it as a tanning booth.

That was back in the days when I was sucked in by the blatant false advertising of the do-it-yourself, labor saving device market. It cost me thousands of dollars before I realized that

none of those gizmos were designed for use by actual people.

Power painters for example. The package shows smiling people painting the outside of their house while dressed up to go to a wedding. I tried it and got paint everywhere. The dog, who is still partly orange, howls when I pick up the power painter now.

I installed a ceiling fan once. Won't do it again. By the time I got done wiring it, the damn thing only had two speeds: semaphore and frappe. One hypnotizes you while the other feels like the house is being buzzed by a Spad.

Then there was the time I sprayed the yard with weed killer. Admittedly, this isn't a mechanical chore but it might as well be. Ever tried reading the instructions on the back of a can of weed killer? They're written in Sanskrit by mentally ill bureaucrats. I ended up estimating, and now my backyard only has two green spots. They are exactly the shape of my feet. The rest of the yard is about as lush as the moon.

Computers? Forget it. I tried the "DOS For Dummies" type books. Still too complicated. What I need is a "DOS For Turnips" book.

The end nearly came when I tried to fix my daughter's hamster with a pair of vise grips.

There is a bright side to being fixit stupid. My wife rarely asks me to fix stuff anymore. She says it's cheaper in the long run to mortgage the house and pay a contractor to come in from France. I listened to her plead with one on the phone just yesterday.

"No, my husband did not try to fix the bathtub first."

D E C K
THE BOUDOIR

The best Christmas I ever had was 1978. That's the year my wife gave me $100 and told me to go buy my own Christmas present.

Incidentally, this was the Christmas after the Christmas that I got a sport coat, which I wore once to church and once to change the oil in the car. Since then, my wife has always gotten me what I wanted for Christmas by letting me shop for it myself.

So, five days before Christmas, I was strolling through a mall with $100 in my pocket and the idea of duck decoys in my head. But minutes before arriving at the sporting goods store, I crossed paths with The Boudoir Boutique.

I think it was the mostly nekkid woman in the Boudoir Boutique window that caught my eye. You don't see that very often in a Utah mall. Her beauty so mesmerized me that it was full half hour before I realized that she didn't have a head or any arms or legs. What the mannequin did have was underwear that looked like it was made out of butterfly parts.

Incidentally, for those of you who don't know, "boudoir" is a French word. And as you might expect from the damn French, it's got something to do with sex. I checked and "boudoir" refers to a place where women walk around in their undies. The word "boutique" is also French and means "expensive as hell."

When I came out of the Boudoir Boutique a short time later, I was carrying a sack that weighed less than three ounces and cost exactly $147. Needless to say, my wife was a little surprised when I gave her my own present on Christmas morning. It came real close to being our last Christmas together because when I finally talked her into trying the present on, I almost had a stroke.

Every year since then, I get my wife something that I really want for Christmas. At first it was difficult. I had to overcome a lot of initial embarrassment. For those of you just getting started out, here are a few tips.

Don't be embarrassed. Directly approach the saleswoman and tell the nice lady what you want. NOTE: How you say this is very important.

A good way to put it is, "I'd like to buy something romantic for my darling wife." Conversely, it's not a good idea to say something like, "Yes, ma'am. I'm looking for women's underwear nasty enough to give a range bull a heart attack."

Trust me on this, you aren't the first man to venture into the lingerie area of the store. Granted, the first guy was probably a pervert but he at least opened the way for the rest of us with our more legitimate sordid fantasies.

Actually, the hardest part about buying lingerie for women is figuring out their size. Most lingerie like chemises, teddies and gowns come in small, medium and large. Which is to say, exactly like most women.

When it comes to this kind of stuff, you do NOT want to buy a large for a small woman. If your normally sized wife slips into something romantic that ends up hanging on her like the drag chute from a F-16, you're in serious trouble.

Nowhere is this more true than when buying brassieres, which, like deer rifles, are sized by caliber. If your wife is a 34B,

don't be coming home with a 38DD outfit. This sort of thing will raise worries in your wife's heart and knots on your head.

Also, never assume that your wife is going to look exactly like the lingerie models in the catalog. These models all have one thing your wife or girlfriend doesn't have: you out of their lives.

ROAD RULES

We leave on vacation in a few days. My wife and I are calling it a vacation even though the kids are coming along.

Now that our daughters are teenagers, we agreed that the travel rules will have to change. Mom says their needs and interests are much different than the time they almost burned down the Magic Kingdom. Dad only knows that they are now way too big to mail home.

Rules are essential when traveling great distances with children. Rules can mean the difference between everyone having a wonderful time and Dad going to prison in a state that may have brought back the death penalty.

It goes without saying that travel rules should be fair. The only reason I bring it up is to point out the exact nature of fair. Namely that there is no such thing. And even if there was, it wouldn't be determined by the guy behind the wheel, who, after two days on the road with children, may no longer be mentally competent.

NO-TRITION: This year, everyone has their own cooler. The kids may put anything they want in their coolers, but whatever

goes in there has to last them the whole trip. If they run out because of poor rationing, or they gave it all to a chipmunk, they don't eat until we get home.

PEST STOPS: No more emergency rest stops that last hours and are really just excuses to goof off and look at boys. Stops will last for ten minutes. Anyone not mostly inside the car when the timer beeps gets left for the wolves.

MUSICK: Passengers have no say over the radio/stereo. The driver (or alternate driver) will decide which radio station the rest of the car listens to. With this rule I hope to avoid another facial tic like I got the year we traveled clear across the United States looking for stations playing Debbie Gibson songs.

MUTTERANCES: Freedom of speech does not exist inside a car 900 miles from home. Forbidden vacation utterances are:

- "She's touching me."
- "I threw up."
- "Can I drive?"
- "I'm bored."
- "Is Dad still mad?

Any hint of "Are we there yet?" will be responded to in the affirmative. The car will then slow to half speed while the petitioner is forcibly ejected to complete her vacation on the side of the road.

CRAMPING: When deciding where to pitch the tent for the night, the tent pitcher (me) will entertain requests from the Vacationing Mom only. Said requests are limited to one per evening and must be expressed before the tent is actually up.

MON-STIR: The Vacationing Dad will make one (1) foray per night to investigate imagined threats. Noises that sound like they are being made by bears, cougars, extra-terrestrials, cows and guys in hockey masks will not be investigated until noon of the following day.

BACKTRAPPING: No matter what we forgot, or how long ago we forgot it, we aren't turning around and going back to get it. We will simply buy/adopt another.

FRIENDS-EEK: Any and all wildlife will be left in place. "Totally cute" life forms that find their way into the car risk becoming "really icky" dead forms the second I find them.

MIRAN-DUH!: When stopped by the police, only the driver of the car may speak. Passengers must stand mute until the police are gone, preferably far out of sight. This will hopefully spare us a repeat of last year's $75 contribution to the Nebraska Department of Public Safety.

FOR-FIT: Before leaving, each member of the vacation expedition must post a cleaning deposit of $50 in cash or kind. Upon our return, anyone who tries to weasel out of clean up chores will forfeit said deposit.

KITCHEN KIDS

I don't know how the dishes get done at your house. At our house, the dinner dishwasher is chosen by a fair and logical method that involves love, a strong work ethic and a handgun. Here's how it goes:

"If you love life, don't forget to wipe down the counters."

I know, I know, you're saying "How can we possibly do this to children?" It's easy. Some proficiency with firearms is a must. That and a grim understanding from the kids that the gun is loaded and you're not kidding.

Oh shut up. My wife and I tried the normal methods to get kids to do the dishes. We offered rewards, praise and even blatant bribes. None of them worked. Ultimately, we decided that the same method my wife used to teach me to help around the house would also work on the kids.

We were right. Kids seem to instinctively know that nothing will screw up their plans for the weekend like a bullet in the knee. They learned even faster than I did. I can even show you the scar.

I don't blame kids for hating to do the dishes. By their very nature, kids are selfish, lazy and inconsiderate. I was there once myself. I was 23 before I was required to help clean up after myself.

Fortunately, I learned to help when the dishes were still fairly easy to do. Back then there was just me, my wife, and our dog, Grim Ripper. The dinner mess—except around Grim's bowl (actually a plastic kiddie pool full of Gravy Train and flies) —could be spiffed up in a matter of minutes.

Then we had kids, three of the little evils. Doing a "good job" on the dishes eventually required the use of a ladder, a steam cleaner, a squeegee, hip waders and six rolls of paper towels. And maybe a bath for the dog. Grim got tired of being covered with strained carrots and ran away.

As they get a little older, say around six or seven, kids still don't want to help do the dishes. Only now it's because they don't eat. The logic is, "Hey, if I don't eat anything all day but half a Pop Tart and some dirt, why should I have to do dishes?"

Kids grow up but that doesn't solve the problem. When it comes to dish mess, teenagers are ten times worse. You don't have to clean food off the walls as much, but you need a search party to round up all the dishes. Today, doing a good job on the dishes also means mowing the lawn and cleaning the basement.

There's another way of getting kids to do dishes besides holding a gun to their heads. Kick them out of the house. My parents tried to do this to me by sending me on a mission. But since we had maids in South America, I didn't wash a dish for two years. Which might explain the cholera.

Ever since we hit on the firearm method of sharing chores, we've noticed a decline in the amount of dishes used to prepare meals. When it's their dish night, our kids don't seem as anxious to have Mom knock herself out making dinner. Instead of lasagna, casseroles or fried chicken, our kids want simple meals —cold cereal, sandwiches or maybe just a handful of dry macaroni.

Sorry, but I've got a lot of getting even to do. Tonight is their night to clean up. So, for dinner, I'm baking a pan of ham glaze (no ham) for nine hours at 500 degrees. Then I'm going to decorate the kitchen with a Salad Shooter. For dessert, we'll set off a cherry bomb in the middle of a German Chocolate cake.

I'd invite you over, but you'd have to help clean up.

L E A S H
LAW

My teenage daughter came home late last night. She was supposed to be home at midnight and instead arrived home at 2 a.m. Which is two hours, unless you happen to be a mother. Then it is physically possible for the time between midnight and 2 a.m. to be 10 hours and 43 minutes.

That's what worry does to your frame of time. Minutes seem like hours. Or at least it does to my wife. I was fast asleep.

This morning, we grounded our daughter until the Second Coming. Not for missing her curfew, but for not calling. In terms of Kirby Family Crimes, not calling is second only to mouthing off Mom within earshot of Dad, doing something to the dog that requires expensive medical attention and misplacing the television remote control.

In our family, kids keeping their curfew is important. Part of proving to your parents that you can be responsible is keeping your deadlines. However, keeping deadlines is not as important as calling us if they're going to be late.

Not calling is worse than being late because two minutes after our kids are supposed to be home, my wife starts thinking aliens got them. Worse, she wakes me up to explain her theories.

It's a maternal thing, the logic of which fathers can appreciate but never duplicate. When the kids are late, official Mom behavior goes something like this:

One minute late—"I'm starting to get worried, dear."

Five minutes late—"Oh, I just know that something bad has happened."

Ten minutes late—"Call the police and hospitals."

Fifteen minutes late—"Why isn't someone dragging the lake and putting up roadblocks?"

Twenty-one minutes late—"I'll have to buy a dress for the funeral."

Anything over 30 minutes late and Mom wants to bring in Mulder and Scully.

Meanwhile, Dad is trying to get some sleep. He has to go to work in the morning. All he really knows is that whatever actually happened to the kids will be best dealt with tomorrow by a person not crazed from the lack of sleep.

It's not that fathers don't care. We do. It's just that a father's official worry clock runs on hours rather than minutes. Furthermore, a father has the added worry of what the lateness means in terms of dollars. If a kid is five hours late, the father is frantic, mainly about what might have been done to the family car.

Parents worry because they know bad things can and sometimes do happen to kids. It's something that most kids haven't clued into. Every kid in the world thinks they're almost immortal if not actually too cool to die.

My daughter naively thinks that she can take care of herself. I tell her that the only reason she believes this is because she isn't familiar with some of the truly evil things lurking out there in the dark. I never tell her that the reason I know about those things is because I used to be one of them.

When I was a teenager, I had a curfew. It was 11 p.m., the local official curfew for juveniles. I never kept it. Somehow, whatever was going to happen to me for breaking curfew—lecturing, beating, grounding—wasn't as important as convincing Suzy Buchowitz to stay out after her curfew.

Parents and teens should talk about curfews. As a kid, I strenuously argued for a curfew of 4 p.m, of the following day. My father put his foot down (barely missing my neck) and said that my curfew would be whatever the law said it was.

Dad's logic was that if the police couldn't trust juveniles to be out after 11 p.m., he damn sure wasn't about to either. Especially since we were talking about me. Having since been a teenager, father and cop, I can say that my father was right. Besides, I know for a fact from my grandma that his curfew was sundown.

My daughter wept and screeched about being grounded. She called her curfew unreasonable and said it was because we didn't trust her.

She finally got something right.

SCHOOL
FOOL

Yesterday was the first day of school. I watched my kids leave
in the morning, each of them happy to be going back after a
long, fruitful summer spent sleeping and watching soap operas.

Just before she left, my daughter said she wanted to get back
to school to see all her friends again. Summer had been long, hot
and boring. "School is cool," she said.

Watching my daughter get on the bus, I decided that I could
afford no more than $500 for a contract hit on my cheating wife.
I'm serious. There's no way that kid on the bus could be mine.

From what I remember, the first day of school was the worst
day of the year. Only geeks, nerds, doodles and screamers actually looked forward to it. Oh, and Mr. Whacker, the principal.
Meanwhile, the sane world seriously considered the alternatives
of self inflicted wounds or the Merchant Marine.

I can't ever remember summer vacation being boring. OK, the
summer I broke a leg and an arm jumping out of Leon's barn loft
with a parachute was almost boring. I spent four weeks in bed
reminding myself that a drag chute designed to slow down a

52,000 pound F-105 Thunderchief will not break the fall of a 85 pound kid.

Generally speaking however, summer was the jewel of a kid's life. It was our due after spending nine months listening to adults rattle on about gerunds, long division and "the following boys will report to Mr. Whacker's office..."

How could summer possibly be boring? Even if your parents made you stay home, you still had your imagination. Add to that a lot of unsupervised time and you had the stuff that dreams (also wars and disasters) were made of.

Not all kids are made that way. When I was a kid, our neighbors went to Disneyland every summer as a reward for behaving themselves during the school year. A real kid doesn't need an artificial environment to have fun. All he requires are a dog, at least two friends of equal or lesser intelligence, a bike and six books of matches.

Going back to school was like going back to jail. Even today, after I've eaten something that has upset my stomach, all I have to do is remember waiting for the bus on Elwood Avenue and the problem invariably resolves itself.

None of this means that school was a complete waste of time. School taught me a lot of things that helped me get thus far in life. They just weren't the things that school intended to teach me.

For example, school tried to teach the importance of authority and cooperation. What I learned is that if a rule sounds stupid at first, it generally remains stupid even after prolonged examination. Furthermore, anyone who enjoys being in a position of authority warrants never ending torment.

School wanted me to read sonnets, essays, treatises and texts. Instead, I learned how to read Mark Twain and Mad Magazine. Not once in my entire life have I ever regretted not developing a passion for Shakespeare.

Other things school tried to teach me were isosceles triangles, tempo and meter, French, objective pronouns, paramecium, four basic food groups and the agricultural resources of British Guiana.

What I actually learned was that I hated all of those things and the Magna Carta to boot. Also that some teachers should have been fry cooks instead. Oh, and that summer school bites.

Now that I think about it, maybe it's a good thing that kid on the bus isn't mine. She may actually go somewhere in life.

SICK OF LEARNING

My daughter got up this morning and said she couldn't go to school because she was sick. It was lie, of course. She just didn't want to go to school.

I knew it was a lie because a) she's a teenager and teenagers are incapable of discerning the truth much less telling it, and b) because I used to pull the "I'm dying, can't make it to school" bit when I was a kid, too.

My wife thought otherwise. Irene sent our daughter back to bed where the girl played Nintendo until her friends came home. Then she went out to play like nothing was wrong. Which, of course, nothing was.

Even by the terms of a Jimmy Carter treaty, this is no fair. I never got off so easy when I was a kid. My dad once made me go back to school three hours after I hit a Ford pickup on a motorcycle. In fact, he drove me straight there from the emergency room.

"Your legs are broken, but you don't have a head injury," he said. "So get back in there and learn something."

I got even with him by not learning a thing and by turning out just like him. Which basically means that when our daughters get sick, whether real (very seldom) or imagined (94.7 % of the time), they always plead their case to Mom, who is both educated and sympathetic.

In our house, pleading woe to Mom works nearly every time. A flushed look and a listless demeanor will get you miles of sympathy, lots of pampering and strawberry ice cream from Mom, and absolutely zip from Dad.

Mainly because Dad always demands proof. None of this "I don't feel good stuff." You gotta show me a missing limb or at least a compound fracture. Only in very rare cases, will I go for projectile vomiting and radiation boils.

Being a dad, I know what's going on in a kid's head. Usually, not very much. But when it comes to a pending math quiz, kids have a genius for turning a sniffle into tuberculosis. The more dubious you are, the harder they try to convince you that they're telling the truth.

Facing a history test, my oldest daughter once tried to convince me that a week-old mosquito bite was actually a fresh bullet wound. Six years later, she still drags her leg around the house whenever she gets sulky.

Actually, I'm not entirely unsympathetic to my kids getting sick. Logic (if not actual empathy) dictates that not all ailments are obvious. In the early stages, for example, it's hard to tell if a kid has the flu.

My wife (and the school board) says that sending a kid to school with a contagious cold or the flu is irresponsible. I say they got it at school and so they can take it back. Why should they stay home and give it to me?

There's another reason why I'm so skeptical. Unlike most men, I work at home. So I see the difference between the way a kid says it is and the way it really is. "I feel yucky" at 7:30 a.m. almost always evolves to "Can I go out and play?" by 8:10. By noon, they're ready to compete in the Olympics.

My wife says it's just because I'm jealous. She's right. This morning, I wasn't feeling too good. In fact, I was pretty sure that I was dying. "Scurvy or dysentery," I told the wife. "I better rest in bed."

Did I get any sympathy? Ice cream? Hell, no. What I got was a lecture about my behavior at yesterday's Superbowl party, followed by a pointed reminder that the mortgage and the car payment were due.

Where's my mom when I need her?

DRIVING
THIS CRAZY

Took my daughter to driver's education yesterday morning. For the record, 5:45 a.m. is a horrible hour to teach kids how to drive like adults. Driving to the high school, this particular adult was so tired that he ran two stop signs and chased a jogger onto a porch.

Lack of sleep notwithstanding, my daughter is more excited about getting her license than the time we told her Leonardo DeCapprio called to ask her out. It was a lie, of course. But what teenager truly appreciates reality anyway?

Few rites of passage are as significant to a kid as getting a driver license. For teenagers, the milestones of life are:

1. Get born.
2. Get potty trained.
3. Get free car.

Conversely, nothing is more significant to parents than a teenager getting a driver license. It means the kid has moved on from being irritating to being dangerous. Parents know that the average kid can barely afford to pay attention, never mind insurance premiums.

According to my daughter, driver's education lasts just a few weeks. The first part is classroom study on the theory of driving. Namely that it should be conducted in such a way that nobody gets sued or killed more than absolutely necessary.

The second part is where the theory is examined practically by placing a test adult in a car with several teenagers. If said teens bring the test adult back alive, they may then apply to the state for licenses to continue doing so.

Maybe it's me, but drivers ed was a lot more involved when I was a kid. For one thing, it lasted an entire semester. And we got to run over people.

1969. John F. Kennedy High School. Drivers ed was held in an airless classroom near the gym. The first part was umpteen weeks of memorizing the Motor Vehicle Code. Anyone who did not know the precise co-efficient of friction for a dry bituminous surface was summarily flopped to Study Hall.

At the end of the classroom portion we were shown several films with daunting titles like "Blood and Asphalt" and "Guts in the Gutter." The idea was to shock us into responsible motoring with scenes of actual traffic gore. All I remember for sure is the girl next to me heaving her lunch into a three ring binder.

Next came the simulators. In a darkened trailer were a dozen mock vehicles connected electronically to a switchboard. We sat in the simulators and tried to mimic the actions of a film. The teacher monitoring the console let us know if the signals from our simulators were in line with what was on the screen. But since the car in the film behaved normally no matter what you did in the simulator, it was hard.

"Driver number six, you just killed that dog."

"Three, you can't parallel park going 62 miles per hour."

"Get out of the lake, nine."

If the football coach was doing the monitoring, we sweated every turn signal. If it was Miss Gollinger or a clueless substitute, we intentionally bore down on film pedestrians. My personal best was eleven, the last one on a sidewalk at 102 mph.

Eventually we drove for real. In a parking lot. Then, after a week of squashing orange cones, we took our finals on the open

highway. Mine consisted of 1.9 miles on Rimrock Road with Coach Johnston's hand clenching the back of my neck. I passed.

Looking back, I would have to say that for all the effort drivers ed failed to prepare me for the most important thing about responsible driving. Namely that it's impossible to simulate gasoline, repairs, insurance premiums and car payments.

Just before I dropped her off, I decided not to explain this to my daughter. Why ruin the moment?

P E T
FRETS

After four years of non-stop begging, my daughter finally got a puppy. We're fools, I know. But when it comes to the things teenagers normally want—drugs, credit cards, pierced noses— a puppy seemed pretty tame.

Or so I thought. Early this morning, the puppy crawled up on the bed and whizzed on me. While I cursed and tried to load the shotgun, my daughter ran in and grabbed the puppy. She hid it in her room until the trauma passed

I wanted to get rid of the puppy then and there. What I really wanted was against the law, but I was willing to settle for dropping it off at the Humane Society at 105 mph.

My wife diffused a potentially serious family fight by reminding me that I have subjected our home to worse pets. She was, of course, referring to Boris, my pet college graduate tarantula who got loose in the house one day. We didn't find Boris for two weeks, during which time my wife and daughters stayed at a motel.

Actually, I found Boris on the third day. He was in with the pots and pans. But we had such a good time laying around and watching John Wayne movies, that I didn't say anything until my wife got tired of restaurant food and sent Orkin over.

Tarantulas are harmless. The most dangerous pet I ever owned was a Great Basin rattler named Frank. My mom made me get rid of Frank after he ate two of my little brother's gerbils that I had put in a box with Frank for safe-keeping.

I released Frank out by Duchesne. That was back in '71. If Frank hasn't been hit by a car while sunbathing on the highway, he's probably 15 feet long by now. I should probably take him a pig or something.

The worst pet I ever owned was in the mission field. Hooper was smelly and abysmally dull. Things got worse after he was hit by a car. But since he was also my companion, having Hooper put down was not an option. So I kept him on the back porch until they transferred him.

The most interesting pet was a 35 pound cat named Gadianton. There was something seriously wrong with Gad. You haven't lived until your cat drags a half-dead weasel into your bedroom in the middle of the night. We had Gad neutered following his third drunk driving arrest. Things calmed down after that.

All of these pets are just memories now but they served to define the rules of pet ownership for this family. If your kid wants a pet, maybe you should borrow them.

- No pet may outweigh the largest member of the family. This prohibits kids from bringing home stuff like ponies, steers, elk and gorillas. Or at least not fully grown ones.
- No pet that can disable a grown man with a single bite. This covers sharks, pit vipers, bears, black widows and alligators.
- Pet must have at least one set of the following: arms, legs, shoulders and hips.
- No pet smaller than a Matchbox car. This includes insects, rodents and some of the sneakier reptiles.
- No pet that requires special living arrangement, i.e. aquarium, pouch, den, hive, or burrow .
- No pet that eats more at a single sitting than the rest of the family put together.
- No pet that assumes it gets a turn with the television remote control.
- No pets that slobber, shed or excrete more than 25 pounds in a single day.

These were pretty good rules until last week. That's when we realized that they cover every animal known to science except puppies.

New rule: No pet that stays alive solely by being cute.

FORWARD TO THE PAST

My daughters, ages 19, 15, 13, say they're tired of listening to me beat up on teenagers. According to them, I've forgotten what it's like to be young because I blame the world's woes on adolescents.

They're right. So let me apologize to idiot teenagers by saying that the reason this country is going to the dogs is because it's being run by old people. I turned 43 last month and it suddenly occurred to me that I'm rapidly becoming one of the problems. The older I get, the more Bob Dole seems like a comrade.

Yup, I've only got a few years left before I become, by law, a full-fledged mature adult, a card carrying, crotchety, old goat—a geezer, a gummer, a codger, a coot. Pretty soon, life is going to be one prolonged miserable spiral down into the abyss of memory loss, ear hair and rock'n' roll aversion.

It's no wonder the world is messed up. People get old and turn into their parents. I mean just look around. Everyone out there screwing things up is over 40 with 70 staring them right in the

59

sagging face. Congress, Clinton, Dole, Yeltsin, Castro—they're all trilobites.

You never see kids strip mining rain forests or pointing nuclear weapons at each other. They're too busy doing stuff that looks like it ought to be a Sunny Delight commercial.

Face it, old people shouldn't be allowed to run governments. How can you possibly be worried about the state of the world and the security of future generations when your primary interest in life is getting enough bran to stay regular?

Old is dangerous because somewhere along the line, suspicion replaces enthusiasm, intolerance overshadows opportunity and propriety becomes one of the Ten Commandments. The same people who once stayed out all night listening to Elvis and Little Richard today can't go farther than 50 yards from a bathroom without suffering from Post-Traumatic Stress Disorder.

I wasn't that worried about old people running things until the other night when we visited some high school friends. After ribbing me about gray hair, they started moaning about their kids coming home late from dates and threatening the fabric of the entire world with their music.

I looked around and to my surprise, the Pepsi Generation had vanished. There in our places were the bloated, wrinkled and bad-breath bodies of our parents—the Preparation H Epoch—the repressive long-toothed mossbacks we once assumed were kin to Hitler. I thought it was only a scary flashback, but it won't go away.

It's not too late for me to decide that I'm not going to be part of the problem. I intend to age gracefully or at least with a certain amount of coolness. I'm not going to sit around fretting about dying without Medicare because when I check out, I'm going to do it needing a haircut, while The Doors drive my eardrums closer to the center of my head.

For the next 20 years, I'm going to live on Ding Dongs, Coke, pizza and MTV. It'll be great until I reach an age where being old is no longer a guessing game you can cheat at with hair dye, false teeth and voting Democrat.

When that happens, I figure that I'll have two choices: either

run for Congress or let my kids ship me to some lock-down care center with curfews and bed checks. The nurses there will make me wear stupid clothes and shave my head in a fashion reminiscent of boot camp. I'll have to eat boring food and hang around a bunch of irritable wrinkle-butts listening to the Carpenters and Pat Boone. Not one person in the whole place will understand me.

Heck, I should be looking forward to it. If I remember right, that's exactly the way things were when I was young.

WEDDING BELL DUES

The big day has come and gone. My daughter got married on Friday. I'm officially the father of the bride. Or, as my wife says, "bother of the fried."

Up front, the aftermath looks pretty bad. I have no money and our house looks like the Easter Bunny went nine rounds with the Addams Family. Meanwhile, my daughter is off being intimate with a guy from Spanish Fork.

There are some pluses. My daughter had a great day. She married as close as possible within her own species and I've now got an extra room in my house that I'm going to turn into a sports den complete with girlie posters, gun racks and a big screen TV. Or probably a sewing room.

Because it was my first wedding, I went into the whole thing dumb. I soon learned that the traditional job of the bride's father is to stand around, dispense money and keep his yap shut. Sort of like an ATM only not as smart and with a bow tie.

Unlike other more sensible cultures, the father of an American bride doesn't get spit for losing a daughter. Scott didn't purchase my daughter. He didn't show up at my house with a new jet ski

and say, "This gift for big chief." Nope. He came over and sat on my couch until I was ready to give him a new jet ski or a hired beating to leave. It ended up costing me a daughter.

What's that you say? At least the father of the bride doesn't have to pay a dowry? You're an idiot. What do think $750 for a dress and $500 bucks for a reception hall was? I paid a dowry. It just didn't go to the groom or his parents. It went to people I don't even know. That's stupider than the idea of a dowry in the first place.

One of the responsibilities of the father of the bride is to have a heart to heart chat with his new son. I had mine with Scott on the day of the wedding. It went something like this:

"Scott, these are the Nineties. It's complicated but basically what that means for us men is that we have to do twice as many dishes for half as much sex. Also, if Christie ever becomes phys-ically abusive, you can have your old spot on the couch back."

The person I felt the most sorry for (and feared) on Friday was my wife. Nobody works harder and cries longer on a wedding day than the mother of the bride. Consequently, you don't cross her. The most gentle mother of the bride in the world would bite the head off Saddam Hussein if he suggested that the nut cups might look better on the left side of the plate.

The actual wedding ceremony took place in Salt Lake City. We drove there in a driving rain storm. The guy who performed the ceremony first had to abuse us with a long talk, all of which went right over the wedding couple's head. He might as well have been talking to a couple of spaniels for all the impact he had.

"Blah, blah, blah, blah, Isaiah, blah, blah, blah, blah, all eternity, blah blah, blah, blah, blah, blah, blah, blah…"

Then there was the wedding breakfast—held at 3 p.m. It was followed by a reception that rivaled the Cherokee Trail of Tears. Every other person who came through the line acted like some-one had shot them in the leg. Fortunately, they all brought gifts. By the time the reception ended, it looked like we had looted a galleon.

When it was all said and done, I sat on the curb and watched my daughter go off on her honeymoon. She looked so happy and beautiful that I couldn't help but think good thoughts.

"One down, two to go."

When my youngest daughter demanded an opportunity to explain to readers the "truth" about my column, I said no. But then I got lazy one day and let her write a guest column. This is the thanks I got.

DAUGHTER OF THE DEVIL

By Ginny Kirby

I would like to give faithful Robert Kirby readers some idea what it is like to be on the other end of his column. So I came up with "The Top 10 Reasons It Bites to Be Robert Kirby's Daughter."

1. I have no social life because of him. Everyone knows he is my dad, so they won't talk to me because what they say could end up in one of his columns. My friends are afraid to come over to the house because they might end up being famous.

2. He can't sign notes. When I'm late for school, I hate having my dad sign the notes because the attendance secretaries keep them for autographs. Worse, I can never forge his signature because they all know what it looks like.

3. I can never do anything remotely stupid because my dad will write about it. Like the time I wrecked my mom's car. I didn't think he would write about that because I felt so bad. Guess what—I was in the paper the next day.

4. He does not understand that it is never "just a column" when it's about me. Like when I told him that writing about the wreck would ruin my social life. He told me to stop whining, that it was "just a column." But when I went to school, the teacher in my fifth-period class passed the column around for everyone to read. Now I'm known as "Crash Kirby" at school.

5. He won't let me be a teenager. Teenagers are supposed to do stupid things. It is how we gain life experience and learn to be responsible. I can never do these things because then I will be in the paper and famous at school. Like the column about me and my sister using too much hair spray. We had to cut way down because everyone wanted to feel our hair to see if it was true.

6. I hate being seen with him in public. Most teenagers don't like to be seen with their parents. As you can imagine, it is ten times worse for me. Whenever we go out, someone always recognizes my dad. They want to know if I really did the stuff he wrote about. I lie and tell them I was adopted.

7. He's boring. We can never go near a bookstore for just a few minutes. If he even sees a bookstore, we will be there for two hours. All he ever does is read. He needs to get a life.

8. He's not that funny. My dad is a geek. Whenever I get into trouble, he thinks he has to come up with something clever to say. But when I'm mad at him, I don't

want to laugh with him. He even makes my mom crazy. We tell him it is not funny when we are mad, but he doesn't get it.

9. Everyone else thinks he's funny. Some of you think it would be great to live with my dad, that all we ever do at our house is laugh. But come and trade places with me. You won't think he's funny. You will be sick of him by the time you leave.

10. He lies all the time. Nothing ever happens exactly the way my dad tells it. He always has to make it worse. I did not leave pieces of my mom's car all over town. There were only three pieces.

Why me? What did I do to make God punish me like this? I pray but get no answers. So, even though I love him, maybe this is hell and my dad is the devil.

STRIFE IN THE FAST LANE

On Friday, my wife and I returned from a fast road trip to California. Because it was supposed to be a romantic getaway, we decided to drive the scenic back roads. We came home insane.

Ever notice how the slowest people in the entire universe are always the people ahead of you? In northern California, these people were driving motor homes. They choked every road, braking at the slightest curve or dip in the pavement as if they were carrying a load of nitro or someone inside was on the can. Every motor home we managed to pass looked like it was being driven by George Burns' father.

This isn't a specific complaint against old people but rather a broad indictment of dawdlers. And the last time I checked, slowpokes weren't a protected group and it wasn't politically incorrect to savage them in the press.

Normal people (you and me and maybe five others) always end up stuck behind someone who isn't sure where they are going, or even particularly concerned about when or if they'll get there.

On the freeway, it's a mom in a mini van driving at a safe but teeth-grinding 49 mph in the fast lane. In the ATM drive up lane, the person ahead of you will be brain damaged and trying to refinance their house. A simple walk through the mall invariably puts you behind people who want to stroll four abreast through a crowd.

It isn't a bad thing to be slow. But it is a bad thing to be slow in fast places like the freeway, supermarket express lanes, fire escapes and jet runways. And if not exactly a bad thing, it's at least a rude thing to park yourself in a doorway, on the stairs, or some other bottleneck place.

Bar none, the slowest people on earth congregate in the foyer of an LDS chapel. No matter how many people need to get out of the chapel after a meeting, some tortoise always decides that the world will end if they don't drop anchor in the middle of the hall and cork up traffic so they can visit.

Maybe the problem is evolution rather than an abject lack of consideration for others. If evolution had been fair, slow people today would have eyes in the back of their heads or doorknobs on their butts. But, hey, the world needs slow people and fast people, if for no other reason than variety. And maybe a food chain.

Some people will say that fast people are actually the inconsiderate ones. If fast people just had patience and understanding, if they would just stop and smell the flowers, the world would be a better place.

Not even. Somebody please explain how the world would be a much better place if everything was either late or never ever got done.

You might think fast people are rude when they're behind you honking and yelling "please for the love of God speed it up to at least 30 mph!" But you probably wouldn't be so understanding of slowpokes if you were in the back of an ambulance on the way to the hospital, or if your Social Security check was delivered by someone who stopped and smelled the roses.

We need some new handicap laws. Slow people should be required to keep right on everything like the freeway, stairs, malls and trains of thought. There should be a turtle check out lane in supermarkets. Fisher-Price should develop an easy to operate ATM for slowpokes. And it shouldn't be against the law to use anti-tank weapons against motor homes.

We need these laws now. Immediately. C'mon, what are you waiting for? Hurry up!

FIREWORK JERKS

I did a bootleg version of the Stadium of Fire Saturday night. Instead of paying $22 to get into Cougar Stadium, I dragged a lawn chair over to the Marriott Center parking lot and watched the show for free.

I couldn't tell you how many people were in Cougar Stadium for the show. I can tell you that everyone else in the whole world was outside. There were more people per square inch than general conference and a Pearl Jam concert together.

Watching the fireworks Saturday night took me back to my childhood. Root beer, mosquitoes, an awestruck crowd, and the time my brother and I made the entire San Bernardino County Sheriff's Department and the U.S. Army mad at us.

Rather than go into the specifics of that dark time, let me just offer some advice. Never fill an empty fire extinguisher with black powder, plug it with a dynamite fuse, and stick it in a stump behind your grandma's garage.

Better yet, when hysterical authorities are running amok because they believe damage to the city was caused by a preemptive nuclear strike, do not tell them it was you.

Stick with legal fireworks. They aren't as awe-inspiring, but they also won't get you into a ton of trouble. Most legal fireworks won't produce mushroom clouds visible in other states, but then they also won't flatten the garages of old women who will flog you with a mop before turning you over to the police.

Yesterday, I bought a bunch of legal fireworks. I got them from one of those little stands downtown; claptrap descendants of the businesses that once sold firewater and rifles to natives. I spent $40 and got a small sack of sparklers, poppers, snappers, squealers and smokers but no whiskey.

To say that I was disappointed would be an understatement. But since statements comparing these cheesy fireworks to cool ones you make yourself were banned years ago by my wife, I won't go into that. Besides, my daughters liked them and I guess that's what's important. Their enjoyment worked out to about $40 worth of ten minutes of fun that made my yard look like the dump.

The Chinese may be tops at making fireworks, but they need someone besides an opium addict writing their advertising and package instructions. Personally, I found the best value for my money in reading the packaging. "Thanking you for not in hand or mouth lighting" and "Please for not eating" were funny, but the best one was "A Void Upon Sitting."

Animal rights activists must not be making much headway in the Orient. I bought a firework called "Flaming Cat Saluting the Heavens" but it was nothing like the real thing. Oh, shutup.

Maybe the weird names Chinese give their fireworks is intentional. Maybe they know that in our heart of hearts, every. American is twelve years old and when we see something called "Leaping Baboon on Fire" or "Two Torched Peacocks Making Merry" we got to know.

My least favorite firework is the snapper, or, as they're packaged this year, "Wolf Pack Bang Snaps, a Fun Trick Noisemaker." The box had a picture of bloody-jawed slavering wolves which I illogically assumed you could produce from any neighborhood dog with sufficient snapper torment. Not even. My dog actually ate a box of snappers and nothing.

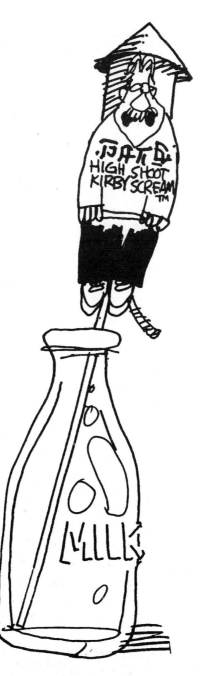

The good part about fireworks is that here in Utah the need for them arrives only twice a year. First is Independence Day on July 4th, the birthday of the federal government. Second is pseudo-Independence Day on the 24 of July when Utahns celebrate our flight from the federal government.

Two is enough. When it comes to imports, fireworks are more expensive per kilo than drugs. Any more celebrating and we'd all be broke.

BONEHEAD EMERGENCIES

On Sunday, I suffered a bad cut to my left index finger. Depending on whose version you believe, I was either wounded rescuing a young woman from a gang of knife-wielding thugs, or I brainlessly cut my finger while trying to make a tuna sandwich. One version sounds better even though it's slightly embellished. The other is my wife's.

I've been hurt before while defending fair maidens. So I knew from experience that my injury was nothing that four rolls of toilet paper, some Scotch tape and a box of Jello Pudding Pops wouldn't fix.

My wife, who has no medical training and rarely gets hurt in a foolish manner, thought differently. She drove me over to the emergency room.

Emergency rooms are disturbing places. There are more stupid people per square foot in an ER waiting room than anywhere else on earth. Oh, everyone who goes to the ER isn't necessarily stupid, of course. Some smart people get hurt accidentally. But

75

for every heart attack victim and injured child, there are ten people moaning in the waiting room because they tried to do something like water ski under a boat dock.

I freely admit to being an ER moron. My trips there have invariably been the result of activity humiliating even to monkeys. That's why I always prepare a more respectable version for my injuries. The last thing you want to admit to someone who will soon be in a position to legally hurt you is that you're wasting their time because you did something foolish.

Lying to ER nurses and doctors has become something of a habit with me. I can't help it. I'm so compulsive about it that on Sunday, when a nurse asked who was bleeding on her waiting room floor, I admitted that I saw an LAPD officer sneak in and squirt the blood from an evidence bag.

Actually, I'm glad I went to the ER. I saw something that made me feel lots better. It's a poster in the waiting room displaying the weird things nurses and doctors have found accidentally inserted into the ears, nose, lungs, stomachs and navels of people so dumb they probably missed being born as sheep by only two or three IQ points.

Among the items on the bonehead board are buttons, unfired bullets, cosmetic applicators, cotton swaps, dry pasta, bugs, coins, paper clips, beans, toilet tissue, nails, string, batteries and, in one really determined case, an adult size toothbrush.

I'm unclear as to the original intent of the bonehead board. All I know is that seeing it made me feel better about my knife wound. Hey, it's one thing to cut yourself making a sandwich and then claim it was actually the result of a gang fight. It's another thing to try and tell an ER nurse that a dozen ninjas held you down and viciously poked a lima bean or a nickel up your nose. Talk about embarrassing.

I also feel less bad for lying about how I got hurt because I was reminded on Sunday that ER nurses lie worse than I could ever hope to.

"This won't hurt as bad as you think," the nurse said as she prepared to inject local anesthetic into my finger.

She was right. It was only a thousand times worse. Instead of

a poke from a needle, it felt like she was trying to saw my finger off with a quarter. That or she was debriding the wound with a badger or a Weed Eater. Curled up in a fetal position, with my eyes tightly shut and shrieking like a teenage girl in labor, it was hard to tell.

Other than that, my wife says I took it like a man.

WINTER BLUNDER LAND

Monday's brief storm left a layer of white on the mountain above my house. As an orthodox snow removal guy, I am waiting fretfully for the first big one of the year. When it comes, I'm moving to Egypt.

If you believe the stuff about La Niña, the first winter storm is supposed to be a doozy. Weather people are unanimous in their predictions. Professional opinions seem to center around the "Kill yourself now" theory.

It's not this bad for everyone. My neighbors are all reformed snow removalists, meaning that they have fallen from the purer faith of removing snow with a shovel. They have snow blowers. Winter mornings in my neighborhood sound like the Ardennes offensive.

I clear my driveway in the manner intended by God: "through sweat of brow and curse of mouth" (as translated from the original Greek). Furthermore, my reward is a celestial one—meaning I will probably die sooner than my neighbors.

The only other person on my street who still uses a snow shovel is Gary, but his faith is manifested by proxy. He has teenage sons.

Granted, having sons is no guarantee that they will shovel snow upon command. For that, you also need an electronic incentive, something along the lines of a cattle prod big enough to ruin the reproductive capabilities in a woolly mammoth.

But at least teenage boys are known to have shoveled snow. The same cannot be said of teenage girls, who, through the cruel biology of just having done their nails, are incapable of shovel use.

I know what you are thinking, that the Smithsonian has an actual 1962 photograph of a teenage girl using a snow shovel. Not even.

Historical research has proven that the girl in the picture—Dawnette Fontinette, 14, of Flat Bug, Utah—is not clearing the family driveway. She is in fact using the shovel to cover her father's body after his heart fell out through one of his pant legs while shoveling a six-foot drift.

This is not going to happen to me. Since God did not give me sons to electro—er, educate about the art of snow removal, I have taken it as a sign that I can buy a snow blower.

For those unfamiliar with snow blowers—probably the same ones still waiting for the results in the Spanish-American War—they are a recent technological invention.

As you know, competition is what drives technology. That's why, shortly after medical science invented the brain embolism and heart attack, someone invented the snow blower. The first one was patented in 1906 as the "De-Lux Automatic Fur Peeler."

While originally intended as a radical method for grooming poodles, it was soon discovered that the Peeler was also capable of throwing onto a neighbor's driveway snow that originally belonged to you. An entire new industry was born, resulting in the need for more cops.

Today, snow blowers come in a wide variety (but three basic) types, all of which are for external use only.

Small snow blowers are great if the amount of snow to be removed is very light. In most cases this amounts to a level of snow meteorologists describe as "imaginary." Do not be fooled by the size. A small snow blower still carries a price tag big enough to trigger your gag reflex.

Medium snow blowers are your best bet, mainly because they are sturdy enough to suckup a frozen-solid Sunday edition of *The Tribune* without slamming the operator back and forth on the driveway in protest.

Personally, I'm going for the large snow blower. The one I have my eye on has a CD player and four-wheel drive. If I get it in red, maybe I can also get my daughters to drive it.

T E N T
TRAILER FLAP

Just got back from the Grand Canyon. Our first vacation of the year came close to being our last.

Because past family vacations have resulted in near death and actual financial ruin, we decided to upgrade our vacation habits. We bought a pop-up tent trailer.

The modern pop-up tent trailer is about the size of a saltine box. It's half trailer and half tent and not much different than the handcart my great-grandfather Korihor Kirby pulled across the plains. The biggest difference is that I pull mine with a GMC while Grandpa Korihor used a team of wives.

Because our trip to the Grand Canyon was cold and rainy, I discovered that the new pop-up trailer sets up exactly like our old tent. To wit: while my wife and daughters wait in the car, I am out in the rain and dark fighting with the canvas like a sailor on a clipper ship rounding the Horn.

My wife reciprocated by cooking me a hot meal on the propane stove inside our new pop-up trailer. Although nothing happened, I suspect the propane stove is where tent trailers like ours get the "pop-up" nickname. Mismanaged, a propane stove will quickly turn a tent trailer into something resembling a fully inflated pan of Jiffy Pop.

According to the manufacturer, our pop-up trailer "sleeps five." This is true if the aforementioned five sleepers happen to be really short and comatose dwarves. I spent the entire first night trying to figure out who came up with the number five. After all, in terms of complete honesty, the manufacturer could just as easily have claimed "sleeps 200." So why five?

It came to me along about dawn that "sleeps five" was one of those foreign metric figures. To get the accurate American number of sleepers, you had to divide the Japanese "sleeps five" by a U.S. conversion factor of 4.5 to get "sleeps one and a very small dog."

A tent trailer is supposed to be sturdier than a tent. Since none of the pop-ups on the market today can be carried in a backpack without giving you a hernia the size of hot air balloon, I guess this part is true.

The sturdy argument was in doubt, however, when a high wind came up Friday night. When that happened, I started wishing for our old tent. See, a tent is at least anchored to something that's hard for the wind to move around—the ground.

In a high wind, the bottom half of a tent trailer squirms and bucks just like the top half, which is to say like Dorothy's house in the "Wizard of Oz" only more so. We spent Friday night wailing for Aunty Em.

But the main reason we bought the tent trailer was because of the bug factor. If a pop-up does nothing more, it at least puts women four feet higher than most bugs, none of which are dangerous unless you happen to be caught in the retreat path of a woman who suddenly sees one.

This is not to say that the bug factor is not an important consideration in family camping, especially if it's being bugged that bugs you the most. After about five hours, a pop-up tent trailer feels like two people wearing the same strait-jacket. This leads to "pop-up fever," which, in our family at least, progresses directly to a high incident rate of injury among teenagers.

At 5,000 bucks a piece, it's hard to afford two tent trailers. This is why a family should never get rid of the tent when they buy a tent trailer. It gives Dad someplace to sleep.

FALL
GUYS

During our trip to the Grand Canyon last week, we went on a geology tour. For those of you who have not been there, the Grand Canyon is so deep you can occasionally see the back of some guy's head in Pakistan.

The park ranger conducting the tour explained at length how the Grand Canyon is composed of various types of rock, and what kind of dinosaurs lived in the canyon 125 million years ago.

Interesting if you happened to be a scientist, which I am not. And judging from the tone and scope of their questions ("Where are the rest rooms?" "How far is it to Flagstaff?"), neither was anyone else in the group.

It takes a trained journalist with a keen mind to know how to force a bureaucrat to tell the real story. I asked the guide how many people get killed every year falling into the Grand Canyon.

The guide said an average of three.

If you were planning on visiting the Grand Canyon, do not be alarmed. The odds that one of the three could be you are pretty slim for two very big reasons.

BIG REASON #1 — Upwards of five million people visit the canyon every year, of which 4.5 million are Japanese.

BIG REASON #2 — Of the people who do fall in, 97.6 percent of them are males between the ages of 18-25.

Never mind rocks and dinosaurs. This was the most important thing I could know about the Grand Canyon. Being 45, married (which makes my gender a moot point), and not Japanese, it therefore was statistically almost impossible for me to fall in.

While actually falling into the Grand Canyon may be a guy thing, it's undoubtedly caused by females. Which is why I am willing to bet that a girl or woman was watching in 100 percent of the falls involving males.

Climbing out on a ledge over the Grand Canyon is not something that can be attributed to a guy's normal lack of smarts. Men are not very bright as a rule, but we're certainly brighter than that. There has to be an outside influence.

It could be beer, but my guess is women. Females upset the natural balance of testosterone in men. As you know, testosterone is that stuff in men that makes us do things like kill other men, kill big animals and invent nuclear weapons to kill lots of both simultaneously. Add a woman to the mix and we become marginally self destructive as well.

For some strange reason that I used to know when I was 18-27 but have since forgotten, guys need girls to notice them. We will do anything to get that notice, including mashing ourselves on a steep part of Arizona.

This kind of attention-getting is most dangerous to young guys because they generally have very little of the stuff that truly impresses women: money. Until they get some, a guy's female attention-getting devices are limited to behavior involving speed, height, weight and wound size.

Old guys usually are married, and whatever money we have belongs to our wives. And since my wife couldn't even get me to go back to the car for some sun block, it's safe to say that I was not about to brave death by climbing out on the edge of a canyon to impress her.

If you're female and find this stuff about guys amusing, this is perhaps a good time to point out that anyone who belongs to a gender that resorts to silicone breast implants as an attention-getting device has no business laughing at another gender for showing off by prancing around on the edge of a cliff.

EXTERNAL USE ONLY

Because my wife worked late, I made dinner. We had cold cereal, canned peas, and Oreos. It was an unorthodox but nourishing meal. Or at least it was for me. I was the only one left at the table by the time we finished saying grace.

My youngest daughter ate dinner at a friend's home. My middle daughter used her allowance and ordered a pizza. My oldest daughter and her husband went out. And when she got home, my wife made herself a grilled cheese.

No one in our house appreciates how much I slave over a hot stove. That's because I don't. I purposely cut as many corners as possible. On the nights that my wife works, the distance between the pantry and chow time is about 30 seconds as the crow flies.

It's not that I don't like good food. I just hate making it, especially for other people. Even more especially for my kids. When it comes to providing nourishment for the ungrateful beasts, I have no tolerance, zero interest, and an apron that says "This ain't Burger King. You get it *my* way or you don't get the [expletive deleted] at all!"

In our house, cooking is definitely Mom's job. This is not because I believe cooking is a woman's job, but rather that I believe cooking is someone *else's* job. Preferably someone who knows what they're doing and perhaps even enjoys it.

When I was a kid, that someone wasn't my mother. I wouldn't say that my mother was the worst cook in the world—mainly because I can't personally vouch for Africa and parts of Russia—but she was easily the worst cook in North America.

Other kids had moms that cooked. I had a mom interested in pottery. My mother had such little interest in cooking that local journalism standards prevent me from describing accurately what we ate. Suffice it to say that today the term "home cooking" holds as much nostalgia for me as the phrase "For external use only."

On the other hand, my wife is a great cook. Our first meal together was cheese and crackers. I almost swooned from the heavenly aroma. The culinary difference between the two primary women in my life is dramatic. It accounts for the reason why I weighed 155 pounds when I got married, and about as much as the polar ice cap today.

When my wife cooks, she prepares food with names like protein, carbohydrates, roughage and calcium. Everyone is happy and healthy because our teeth don't fall out from advanced scurvy. When I cook, the family comes slouching to the table like the cast from *Mutiny on the Bounty*. My food has names like "sodium benzoate" and "fillers."

This is not to say that only women can cook. I know some men who are excellent cooks. What? Yes, men who drive trucks, rarely comb their hair and don't live in apartments with ferns. My dad is one of them. He passed on to me his culinary skill: meat + big fire = dinner.

Unfortunately, since there's this thing called nutrition (and another thing called the Division of Family Services), barbecue can legally account for only a small percentage of a growing child's daily requirements. They also need hard-to-fix stuff.

A good family cook has to know about stuff like fresh broccoli, cauliflower, spinach, as well as non-flammable (prissy) ways of preparing them. A low maintenance cook like me knows that you can get all the benefits of stuff like that from a pill shaped like Fred Flintstone.

It's an age-old argument in our house. My wife says that if I made more money, she could stay home and cook for the family. I say that if she stayed home and cooked more, the kids would be healthy enough to hire out as cheap farm labor.

U P O N THE ROOF TOP

This morning, my wife asked me for a divorce. Oh, she didn't come right out and use the D word. She's much too subtle for that. What she said was, "When are you going to put up the Christmas lights?"

Longtime veterans of marriage to women know that "today" is the proper answer to such a rhetorical question. What I said was, "Just as soon as I finish killing Herb."

Every neighborhood has a Herb. On my street, it's Herb Mote. Most of the year, Herb is a nice guy. Easy-going and soft spoken, he loans me tools and helps me fix stuff before my wife gets home. But every year, sometime around Thanksgiving, Herb turns into the anti-Christ.

Herb is the first guy to put up Christmas lights. To his credit, he does a great job. What the rest of the men on the street can't figure out is why. Not only is Herb's wife much smaller than he is, none of us have ever seen her hit him with anything larger than a crock pot.

Herb dragging lights around on his roof is the first sure sign of Christmas in the Spring Hills subdivision. This wouldn't be a big deal if our wives didn't notice, but they do. Mainly because when he's finally done, Herb's house is so festive that you can see it from Alpha Centauri.

After that, it's non-stop spouse reminders like, "Today would be a good day to put up the lights, dear," and "Let's make Christmas really special this year." While these all sound harmless enough, men know that they are just different ways of saying, "Go up on the roof and hurt yourself."

I didn't always know this. When I was a kid, I believed my mom when she said that Christmas lights were designed to show Santa Claus where to land. After I got married, I believed my dad's shouts from the top of the house, "Lousy #@&*! lights!"

As a veteran Xmas light guy, I offer this simple checklist as a way of making the job easier.

SAFETY — Getting up on the roof is not the hard part. That would be the ground, which you want to avoid returning to without the use of a ladder. Since Christmas lights typically go around the part of the roof known as "the edge," there is no way to avoid this hazard. You can, however, soften your fear with lots of insurance and/or eggnog.

PREPARATION — Untangle and test the lights before dragging them up on the housetop. This is very important because no matter how carefully you stored the lights last Christmas, they will be snarled again this Christmas. Furthermore, half of them will not work two-thirds of the time. The edge of a roof is the wrong place to start wishing that you had never been born.

ARRANGEMENT — Because of gender differences, this may be the most difficult part of Christmas lights. As a rule, women want the lights to be symmetrical in appearance. For those of you thinking "Huh?" right now, "symmetrical" actually means "the way Martha Stewart would like it." For this a guy will need a calculator, a sextant, lots more eggnog, and the patience of the dead.

MAINTENANCE — Just because the lights are up and you are down does not mean that you can forget about them. Lights burn out. For some reason incomprehensible even to scientists, the person not responsible for climbing on the roof will also be the same person most bothered by the fact that one light in 5,000 is not working.

REMOVAL — Depending on how good you are at watching and analyzing the weather, taking down the Christmas lights is something that can be postponed until the end of July.

CHRISTMAS MOURNING

If yours is the average American family, Christmas Day started sometime before 3 a.m. You probably missed it, but your children did not.

A youngster's Christmas begins in stages. For kids, there is the actual, the technical, and the official start of Christmas, none of which have anything to do with laws laid down by church, science or government.

When I was a kid, the actual start of Christmas was whenever I popped awake, normally around midnight, with sweaty palms and an irregular heartbeat. Something about the house was different. I knew that Santa had been there.

Could I do anything about it? No. For kids, there is no worse torture than the time between actual Christmas and official Christmas. You lay there feeling your muscles atrophy and the onset of bedsores. The Second Coming is like the Grand Prix compared to this.

Christmas technically starts the moment kids get out of bed (the first time). Following a brief reconnoiter to the front room to make sure that Santa did in fact make an appearance, plans begin to bring about the official start of Christmas, preferably without drawing shouts or gunfire from their parents.

Official Christmas is when kids can lay hands on what is legally theirs without incurring the wrath of parents, who insist on being there at the beginning, while at the same time wasting the best part of Christmas by sleeping through it.

No kid in his or her right mind starts Christmas without official permission. I tried this once. It just happened to be the Christmas my dad got an 8mm movie camera. Preempting his debut as a director caused us to have a Sam Peckinpah Christmas instead of a Walt Disney one.

One year we tried caroling my parents awake, the idea being that if we awakened them in a festive manner, they would be happy to get up. We crept into the master bedroom, inhaled deeply, and began braying, "Jingle bells, jingle bells..."

My dad, still half asleep, reared out of bed and bit a chunk out of the door frame, narrowly missing my brother's head. That year, Christmas officially started five hours late. Around sun up as I recall.

Christmas teaches children subtlety, something not naturally a part of their makeup. The best way to wake parents up is gradually. Flushing the toilet 50 times works. So does getting the youngest sibling to cough non-stop. Lighting matches is good. No parent can sleep through a whiff of smoke. Hey, whatever it takes. These are desperate times.

Before the advent of caller ID, it was possible for kids to telephone their parents from downstairs, and hang up when they answered groggily. Then, rubbing their eyes and yawning, kids could stumble into the bedroom and ask innocently, "Was that Santa Claus?"

Now that I'm older, I understand Christmas morning from a parental frame of mind. Namely that no matter how late I stayed up to put presents together, I'm not going to be able to sleep in. I've tried everything and it doesn't work.

Probably because my children have developed their own way of waking me up. They learned long ago that the old man cannot

sleep while being stared at. This morning there were four sets of eyes at the foot of my bed. Three belonged to my daughters, the other to the dog, who had no idea what was going on other than it was dangerous.

Now that Christmas is officially underway, the kids can handle it from here. Ignore the mess and the noise. Go take a long nap. You are going to need all your strength for New Year's.

H A I R
CARE

Call me a thrill seeker. Last week, I let my daughter cut my hair. True, she is going to haircutting school. But I have grounded her about 50 times during her life, so there was no guarantee that any of this skill would find its way to my head.

Getting a haircut in the '90s is risky anyway. These days male hair rivals female hair for the amount of attention it receives. It didn't use to be that way. When I was younger, male hair only had two looks, neither of which required a great deal of upkeep.

I remember when a haircut cost 50 cents. For four bits the barber sheared your head and whacked the back of your neck with a whisk broom. Ninety seconds tops.

This, of course, was back in the '60s when my dad was in the Army. For my brothers and me, a trip to the Post Exchange barber was like being dragged to the guillotine.

"I want these boys to look like men," Dad would tell the barber. "Tighten up those sidewalls and trim the backs danger close."

My brothers and I knew what was coming, and to suffer in

silence. When you are 10 years old, you can't argue with someone whose idea of cool hair looks like something you would expect to see sticking out of a hatch on a Tiger tank.

Eager to please, the barber would take the sidewalls up over the top of our heads. He got a total of a buck for ruining our lives. Mom would place us under suicide watch when we got home.

It wasn't until high school that I could stick up for my own head. Partly to make up for all those slash and burn haircuts, but mainly just to drive my old man nuts, I chucked the Vitalis and turned my head into a rain forest.

Eventually, I hit upon a style of my own. Good grooming consisted of combing my hair back with my fingers to rid it of bugs and other debris. Sounds gross but that was how I found my missing Jethro Tull tickets.

Since then I still have managed to get a few really bad haircuts. The first one was at the Ft. Jackson Reception Center in South Carolina where a drill sergeant grabbed the back of my coif and hauled me to the head of 600-yard haircut line.

"Give Daisy Mae here a Yul Brynner special," he shouted to the barber.

Next was the missionary haircut I got *after* entering the LDS mission home in Salt Lake. Despite the fact that I'd had four haircuts in the past week, my hair was technically still too long to serve the Lord.

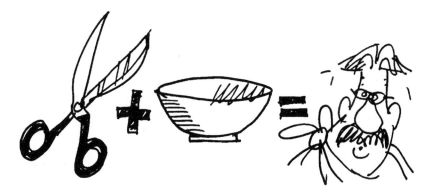

Sitting in a chair near Temple Square, the barber confided to me that he could see the hesitation marks in my hair, and that he would be gentle. Still, it pained me to watch him turn me into an insurance salesman.

Although I don't have long hair anymore, my head is still the product of another time. Parted down the middle, finger combed and then ignored. Like my old man's flat top was in his, it's the style of my generation.

Things are much different today. Even though his hair is much shorter than mine, my son-in-law Scott spends about as much time on his hair as my daughter Christie spends on hers. It involves mousse, spritz, gel, teasing and fussing to get just the right look.

Afterward, Scott's head looks like something you would expect to see poking out of the hatch on a UFO. He got a haircut last Sunday that took three hours and made our dogs hide under the deck.

I don't even want to think about the kind of heads my grandsons will have.

D O G DOC

I took my dog to the vet yesterday. Even though I lied and told her we were going to Denny's, Scout suspected the truth. She started howling as soon as we pulled off the highway.

I hate going to the vet almost as much as Scout. She hates it because it usually involves pain. In her two years, Scout has been hit by an ATV, snake bit, kicked by a horse, and suffered assorted cuts to her tail, feet, nose and tongue. The vet once had to surgically remove a cat from her head.

The main reason I hate going to the vet is because of the wait. I've spent at least a year of my life in medical waiting rooms, and veterinarian offices are always the worst. It's not that the vet keeps me waiting long. I just figure that any time spent with a terrified and shedding 100 pound dog in your lap is too long.

This particular visit involved a toe which Scout had cut while trying to climb a telephone pole after a cat. The cat probably thinks it got away by walking the telephone wires out of sight in the direction of Spanish Fork. What really happened is that Scout got slowed down when she caught her toe on a nail.

"You promised we would never come back here," Scout said. "Remember when I got that weasel stuck in my throat? You said it would be the last time."

"Shut up," I replied. "The only thing holding your toe on is a little bit of hair."

"Doesn't hurt a bit," Scout said. She whipped through her entire repertoire of wiener earning tricks—sit, lay, speak, beg, roll over, shake, and The Twist—in two seconds. "See? Now can we go?"

I think the thing Scout hates the worst about the vet's office is being lifted off the floor and placed on the examining table. Doc Davis' table is made out of formica and has about as much traction as Rush Limbaugh's heart. The same dog who will climb a ladder to chase birds off the roof of the house is terrified of being four feet off the ground on a slippery table. She'll skate around on it with her claws like a fat Tanya Harding.

Then there's the shots. Can anyone tell me why a dog—who unless we tie her up will brainlessly go nine rounds with the Roto Tiller—would be afraid of a needle?

Leaving the vet's with six stitches in her toe, Scout admitted that it wasn't as bad as she thought it would be.

"Speak for yourself," I said. "I'm the one who had to pay the vet."

"Yeah, but we got even. Did you see me tear off his shirt?"

Dog owners know that you reach a point where you wonder if the dog is worth it. Over the years, Scout has cost me big in shots, stitches, surgery, spaying, pills and a tummy tuck that she insisted she had to have after that male black lab moved in down the street.

Driving home, I was sure I wouldn't miss Scout if I told her we were going to Denny's and instead took her to the dog pound. There would be no more vet bills, no more mad neighbors over at my house complaining about how Scout dug a hole in their yard so deep they can hear Chinese being spoken. Best of all, no more dog catcher at my house claiming that Scout is a dog Dillinger.

This morning, I went for a walk by myself. Once I got out of earshot of Scout's howling (2.3 miles) it was very peaceful. I had

time to think about my decision. I decided to keep Scout. Somehow, when you do it solo, cat chasing, cow baiting and digging hysterically for gophers just isn't the same.

INTO THE BAD LANDS

Ray and Doug left ten minutes ago with about a dozen scouts. They'll be back in a week.The scouts will be exhausted, starving and only slightly dirtier than they would be if they'd spent an equivalent amount of time snorkeling in a dump. Ray and Doug will be all of those too, but they won't care because they'll also be insane.

Watching them load up across the street, I briefly considered feeling sorry for Ray and Doug. I decided against it. If I know what happens on scout hikes, then they certainly should. After all, they did the exact same thing last year. It's one thing to feel sorry for people who can't help themselves and another to waste your sympathy on people smart enough to know better.

Most of my own scout hikes are remembered with some degree of fondness. Mostly by my parents who were glad to have me gone for a week, even if, or especially because, a bear might eat me. I have fond memories of lugging a pack the size of a swamp cooler through country shunned even by Bedouins. I have them because I was young and time heals most psychological wounds.

I didn't really understand just how bad scout hikes were until I became an adult and found myself volunteered to lead a group of boys into the hinterlands for a week.

The time was 1976. Walt and I agreed to lead a troop of scouts on a 50-mile hike through a piece of Southern Utah that has never made it into any tourism handbook because it looks a lot like Hell on a bad day. Walt did it because he was a lifetime scouter and wanted his Silver Beaver before he died. I did it because I liked Walt. Or I did before the scouts turned him into a wild-eyed, pistol-waving lunatic.

Only a group of 15-year-olds can take a self-assured business man and in the space of five days turn him into a maniacal dictator with a seething contempt for the human race. They do it a little at a time.

First, scouts always bring more gear than they can possibly carry. They discover this fact about 400 feet into a 50-mile hike, or say twenty minutes after the last vehicle has departed. Within two miles, adult leaders are packing roughly eight times their own body weight and carrying the wimpiest scout in their arms.

Next comes food. I've seen scouts eat the tires off a Hostess truck and ask for seconds. Seriously, scouts may look small, but they need to eat every 18 minutes. So, unless the food is closely guarded with automatic weapons, scouts will eat it all on the first day. Usually before noon.

Most aggravating perhaps is the natural scout hunger for adventure. This always comes at the expense of the adults accompanying them. It's considered negligent to let bears eat scouts even if said scouts attacked said bears first with illegal fireworks. Which means getting between the bears and the scouts.

But if you don't let them have adventure, scouts become dangerously bored. This gives rise to 50-mile hike pranks, the humor of which is very subjective. It normally involves attempts to get adult leaders to cry by squirting toothpaste into the last of the potable water, striking them in the face with a horny toad fired out of a slingshot, burning up their hiking boots or exploding a can of pork and beans in their sleeping bag.

To my knowledge, Walt never got his Silver Beaver. Years later, I saw a picture of him in an abnormal psychology textbook. He looked happier.

Ray and Doug will be back in a week. Or what's left of them.

DOGGING CATS

One of the things many readers do not know about *Salt Lake Tribune* editorial cartoonist Pat Bagley is that he owns a cat. While in normal circumstances such a statement could be construed as libel, I bring it up only to make a point.

The point is that despite this character deficiency, Pat and I are good friends. Rarely do we allow the dog/cat issue to become a problem between us. When it does, we talk about it until Pat concedes or suffers a head injury.

Said issue recently came up in the middle of the night. Because of a late meeting, I was staying over at Pat's house. Around 3 a.m. I woke up with Pat's cat on my face. Specifically a yellow 15-pound ringworm farm named Tiger.

Badly congested sinuses was my first vague thought. Next was that I had somehow managed to fall asleep face down in Big Foot's laundry hamper. The truth was far more horrible.

Pat now insists that I owe him $800. Half for vet bills and half to repair the damage caused by me trying to put Tiger outside without opening any doors or windows. I say the fact that Pat lived through the rest of the night more than makes us even.

It's a moral issue, really. Dogs are simply better than cats.

Your average dog is smarter than two-thirds of the human race, and way more fun than any cat even if said cat was drunk and had just gotten paid.

This blatantly specie-ist utterance will no doubt anger cat lovers. So I want the record to clearly show that I have never condoned violence against cats who did not first cause me a case of dry heaves.

Cat lovers will claim erroneously, that cats are just as cool as dogs. Hardly. My dog Scout sleeps with me and never forgets her manners. She brings in the paper, barks at strangers and never gets sick. Scout once ate most of a chicken coop and all she needed by way of medical attention was a couple of Tums.

Conversely, Tiger will eat only food prepared by French chefs. He is conceited, doesn't know a single trick and recently was the cause of a great deal of damage to the interior walls of his owner's house.

We are going to settle this cat/dog debate right now by taking a little test. It's multiple choice, so even cat lovers should be able to get at least a couple right. Here goes:

Animal that can catch a Frisbee in midair:
a) dog   b) cat   c) beaver.

Animal best equipped to help police track criminals through a swamp:
a) cat   b) dog   c) giraffe.

Animal known for keeping burglars away:
a) dog   b) cat   c) box turtle.

Animal that will bring in a newspaper on command:
a) cat   b) dog   c) platypus.

Animal that will pull a travois:
a) dog   b) cat   c) really buff frog.

Animal with most *Reader's Digest* accounts of saving children from drowning:
a) cat   b) dog   c) Cornish game hen.

Animal that will jump out of a boat and bring back a duck:
a) dog   b) cat   c) musk ox.

Animal that has been shot into space (legally):
a) cat   b) dog   c) small elephant.

Animal least likely to get stuck in a car's fan belt:
a) dog   b) cat   c) another cat.

Animal best suited for savaging door-to-door sales people on command:
a) cat   b) dog   c) pit hamster.

If you answered dog 10 times, you are brilliant and probably over qualified to be a veterinarian. If you answered "cat" even once, you have

    a) difficulty coping with reality   b) few friends
    c) one or more cats   d) all of the above.

HARD WATER DEPOSITS

Whenever I've been mean to my kids, they try to even the score by getting me to take them to the water park. I always say no. My kids overcome this situation the same way yours probably do. They go and get Mom. Then I shut up and we go to Seven Peaks.

Actually it isn't the money that makes me avoid water parks. It's that I'm 42 years-old. Water parks aren't made for people my age.

Water parks are made primarily for kids. After all, the slides, waves and spouts are exactly the sort of things kids try to recreate in the bath tub. Any parent who ever wondered how a six-year-old taking a simple bath can get shampoo on the roof of the house knows this.

The only parts of water parks made specifically for adults are the parts that say Visa and Mastercard. And maybe the first aid station.

It's understandable that kids are attracted to water parks. Seven Peaks looks like something Huck Finn might have dreamed up if he'd lived in this century on a diet of airplane glue and mushrooms. The only liquid there that moves as lazy as the

Mississippi is in some old lady's Thermos. Everything else moves like it was being used to put out an oil field fire.

The unwritten goal of any water park seems to be to convince you that you're having the time of your life while at the same time trying to drown you. They swamp, douse and shoot you through tubes until you feel like a kidney stone being passed. It's a real scream unless you're old enough to know better and dumb enough to have once done it.

The first time we went to the water park, my kids talked me into trying out the tallest slide. The sun must have gotten to me because I finally agreed. I followed my kids over to a tall wooden tower where we stood in a line that was slightly longer than the one when I got drafted. Then we climbed stairs for 20 minutes. When we finally reached the top, I had a nose bleed and a headache.

"It's okay," the slide attendant said when he saw me looking with horror down the chute. "You just lay there and let the slide do the rest."

I took no comfort in this advice considering that I'd heard something like it before at Ft. Benning. From where we were standing, we were looking down on nearby foothills. But the kid was right, the slide did the work. Two seconds after flopping down in the chute, I went down the slide with all the grace of a buffalo pushed out of a helicopter.

The ride lasted five seconds tops. I remember a lot of feminine screaming that my wife later said was me. And when I finally got to the bottom, the thrill still wasn't over. I needed the help of a tow truck to rearrange the backside of my swimming suit.

Now when we go to Seven Peaks, I just sit by the side of the pool and ogle the women in bikinis. Frankly, this is the only part of a water park made for middle-aged men with mortgages and love handles. It's also proof that I can be a water park thrill seeker, too.

If my wife happens to be around, it can also be ten times more dangerous than the slide. Also, given the shape of my heart and the shape of some of these women, I could be dead long before my wife actually got to me.

WEDDING BELLS II

■ attended the wedding of a close friend last week. It was the second marriage for both bride and groom. The groom was scared, the bride happy.

About 25 people attended the ceremony which lasted maybe half an hour, including the part where Al forgot what he was supposed to say. It was a perfect wedding. Short, private, and both parties were old enough to know better if they so chose. Afterward, everyone went over to the happy couple's house where we ate dinner and watched the Falcons win.

I'm not an emotional person but I wept through the ceremony. If Al and Linda's entire hitchment including the ham and side bets on the Falcons cost more than 150 bucks, I'm a Martian. Conversely, my daughter's wedding cost me slightly more than what a Superbowl quarterback makes in a season, including endorsements.

Not that I begrudge my daughter the money. Marrying her off was cheaper in the long run than keeping her around. I just don't get the difference. Why can't first time newlyweds be happy for less like veteran newlyweds?

Forget the money. Lets just talk logistics. Why do people getting married for the first time have to invite everyone in the phone book? Al and Linda's wedding was just the right size. Relatives, a few friends and only one Broncos fan.

Most Utah weddings have become ridiculous. I've received maybe fifty wedding invitations in the last year. Most of the time I haven't the slightest idea who's in the picture. Nor can I figure out my connection with the betrothed by reading their pedigree.

"Mr. and Mrs. Herbert Gumwaddle are pleased to announce the marriage of their daughter, LaMeesha Dawn, to Brad, son of Mr. and Mrs. Lawrence Stupenagle."

When I got this one, it took me two days to deduce that I'd never met LaMeesha Dawn, Brad or Mr. and Mrs. Gumwaddle. Nor had I ever clapped eyes on Mrs. Stupenagle. Eventually it dawned on me that Lawrence Stupenagle was "Stoop"—the guy who drives the garbage truck in our neighborhood.

What kind of gift do you get for the son of someone you hardly even know? In Utah, it's candy dishes or cutlery. At least that's what it was when Irene and I got married in 19-never mind. We received two-hundred candy dishes and enough butcher and steak knives to arm every tribesman in Somalia. Considering that in the first three years we both gained weight and fought like a couple of wolves, maybe the gifts were exactly what we needed.

Still, it would be a whole lot easier on everyone if receptions charged an optional admission, say a buck a head for anyone who chose not to bring a gift. Guests could show up, sign the book, and pop five bucks into a box to see the bride and groom and impoverished parents of each. No more wandering aimlessly around K-mart an hour before the reception. Better still would be the ability to charge your reception attendance fee on a credit card. The guest register could even be a book of Mastercard slips already made out with the names and amounts.

Best of all would be a 1-800 number where you didn't actually have to show up at the reception and stand in line but could simply call in your best wishes to the happy couple for only $5.95 a minute.

Granted, most invitations serve more as notices that someone you barely know is getting married as opposed to being actual invitations to show up and bring something of heirloomable quality as a gift. The trouble is that it's hard to tell which category you fit into.

I should stop complaining about how expensive my daughter's wedding was. After all, it was probably cheaper than getting divorced. Not her. Me.

RISE
AND WHINE

Humans face a common moment of truth every day. For some, the moment is harder than others. It's when you make the decision to get out of bed.

Most people hate getting out of bed before they actually want to, say around 2 p.m. The fact that we get up before we want to is a process of conditioning. It certainly isn't natural. Getting up before it's biologically time to do so first happens when a person is young. Say about 18 months. Babies wake up because they're wet. It's hard to sleep when a water bed consists of a soaked Pampers. Also, when you've slept 35 of the last 40 hours, you can't sleep anymore.

Eventually, you start getting up because of rage. It happens during the teenage years, when your mom stands at the bedroom door and says, "You're going to miss the bus" over and over until you want to explode. After an hour of this, there's no point in trying to sleep any longer. You're so mad you could eat a bus.

For me, getting up because of rage lasted until the Army got me. Drill Sgt. Valentine didn't stand at the door of my room and scold me like Mom. The first time he caught me sleeping in, Valentine simply heaved the entire double bunk with my bunkie and me in it over onto the floor. Then he grabbed us by the waistbands of our skivvies and dragged us into the latrine.

"What if I'd been the Viet Cong?" Valentine bellowed, flinging us into a cold shower. As long as I was asleep when it happened, having my throat cut by a VC sapper seemed a preferable alternative to an ice water shower at 5 a.m. However, this was something I wisely kept to myself. While in the custody of Uncle Sam, I never slept in again. I couldn't. At 4:55 a.m., my eyes clicked open and my heart started pounding. I got up on time out of fear.

Later, in the mission field, I encountered getting up out of guilt. That's when a companion or some pin head of a zone leader holds forth on the impossibility of sleeping in an extra ten minutes and loving Jesus at the same time.

"If you really loved the Lord, Elder," a companion said to me, "you wouldn't be sleeping in like that. Breaking the rules is a sin."

"And if you really loved the Lord, Elder," I replied, "you wouldn't be trying to kill yourself by bugging me about it. Suicide is a worse sin."

"Oh, yeah? Well if you really loved the Lord…"

When I came home, got married and had kids, I encountered getting up out of obligation. I had to get up and go to work 5-6 days a week in order to be able to sleep in one morning.

I got up and went to work on time because if I didn't, I'd get fired. And, as all married men know, when that happens there's really no point in ever going back to bed again for sleep or anything else. It won't do you a bit of good.

Now that I'm getting older and don't have to be to work at any particular time, I'm still getting up early. I've nearly come full cycle. If I don't get up at 4 a.m. and crawl into the bathroom, I'll be sorry.

I'm not afraid of getting older because eventually I know I'll be headed for the Big Sleep. I'll be dead and, barring any scientific breakthroughs, no one can get me up. Or so I thought. I forgot about the Resurrection. The way it's looking, I won't be dead five minutes and someone will be blowing a horn to get up. My wife says not to worry. I won't be called until the very last. Until then, the rest of you keep the noise down.

FLASHBACK PAYBACK

Rumor has it that when you die, your entire life flashes before you. I hope not. I just watched mine and it wasn't pretty.

Last month, my parents converted all their 8-mm home movies to video. After some really demented editing, the three hour epic was passed on to their kids as individual Christmas presents. (Rated G, turkey).

After watching the videos, mostly disjointed scenes of holidays, vacations, picnics and assorted military installations we called home, my conclusions are this: a) my father was no photographer, b) I should have tormented my little brother more, and c) there should have been a law preventing our parents from having children in the first place.

In a few hours, I watched myself go from toddler to teen to tired. At the end, I thought, "What a gyp." Not because of the quality but rather because I watched my life zip by and dwindle down to what I am today without warning.

This doesn't mean the quality of the video was great. In fact, it gave me a headache. Mainly because my dad kept fiddling with the focus, zooming in and out on us like a drunk trying to film bugs. Twenty-five years and he never figured it out. Also, the lighting was so bad that much of the video appears to be of pajama-clad kids space walking.

The sound is horrible. With rare exceptions, it's impossible to understand what's being said. My dad's idea of capturing quality sound was to put the microphone as near to the speaker's tonsils as possible. A clip of my siblings and me singing Christmas carols sounds like a troupe of walruses belching helium.

The brightest star of the Kirby epic is my mother, periodically caught on film in Spain, France, New York and Boise, Idaho. I grew up oblivious to the fact that there was a time when my mother turned men's heads. If I live to be a million, I'll never understand why she married a guy whose idea of haute fashion was a crew cut and a bow tie.

Lest it seem that I'm being too hard on my father, let me point out that the person who really gets trashed in this movie is moi. Whatever respect or fear I may have once inspired in my kids is gone after seeing me with a buzz cut, in diapers, learning to ride a bike and wearing disco clothes.

The special moments of my life captured on film for posterity were greeted with guffaws and shouts of "dork," "dweeb," "nerd," "troll," and "What a loser!" The worst was, "Saturday Night Fever wannabe, eh, Dad?" I can't even make eye contact with them anymore.

Fortunately there were also some positive scenes. My kids loved the dog I had when I was 10. They thought our trips to the castles of Europe were neat. It blew their minds that Granny was once gorgeous.

Best of all, my kids got to see what their own mother was like before time, pregnancy, and raising kids marked her for life. This was my favorite part, too, although it left me wondering what a woman like that could have ever seen in a guy who considered platform shoes haute fashion.

Even as I write this, I can hear my kids laughing hysterically

in the TV room. I know it's not Robin Williams or Steve Martin making them laugh. They're laughing at my life, scenes of me getting bucked off a teeter-totter, being potty trained, running around naked with a cap gun, or acting tough with my hood friends. It's entertainment at its worst.

I'm learning to deal with it, though. At this very moment, a dozen video cassettes of my own kids line a shelf in my office. It's only a matter of time until I have teenage grandkids.

DEATH BEFORE HIS HONOR

In the *USA Weekend* magazine that came with the Sunday *Herald*, the cover story was all about making a personal choice of dying. Namely, who gets to say when it's your turn.

The article included a survey which claimed that 57 percent of Americans now approve of their doctor helping them check out. Oregon recently passed Measure 16, their Death With Dignity Act. The measure so angered Oregonians that now half of them want to kill the other half. People in favor of death with dignity say they have a right to choose when it's time to die. They'd rather be with God than in a hospital waiting to die.

Opponents of death with dignity say such measures send false messages to the elderly and teenagers. A euthanasia law will cause the elderly to believe that no one wants them around, while teenagers will look on it as a sign that life is more hopeless than they previously thought. Actually, the reverse is true. Being old

is hopeless while being a teenager means that most reasonable people think you'd make better sense in a box underground.

Personally, I'm against doctor assisted suicide. Not because I think it's anybody else's business when I die, but because like everything else we've done as a species, euthanasia will eventually get out of hand.

Choosing to die is an intensely personal matter. Right now if a doctor helps you, it's usually because he respects you as a suffering human being, or because he's trying to cut back on the number of patients.

Legalize euthanasia and overnight people will be trying to make money off it. Euthanasia centers will pop up all over, ranging from the chic to the cheap. Sears will have a booth next to their insurance stand. 7-11 will sell little do-it-yourself pills that come with a free Big Gulp. Salesmen will come knocking on your door offering to kill you for 20 percent off.

Worse, there'll be commercials on television telling people where they can get deals on being killed. "That's right, ladies and gentlemen. At Oblivion Bob's we can make the world go away for only…"

Frankly, I wouldn't want to go to some discount suicide place where their idea of easing me into death would be to hit me with a hammer when I wasn't looking. I'd much rather check out in a nice, expensive hospital with a snootful of drugs and Enya crooning in the background. The question is which one will I be able to afford when it's time?

Then there's the time part. When it comes to wanting to die, few people are all that rational. There have been times in my own life when euthanasia seemed the only option.

The first time was when I was six and accidentally wet my pants on the playground in front of LeAnn McDermott. Talk about wanting to die. If there'd been a Euth-Center across the street I would have sprinted right over with my lunch money.

Finally, the government will come up with a Death Tax. You won't even be able to get away from them by dying like you can right now. No way. They won't let you die until you fill out a form and give them a bunch of money. Heck, they'll keep you on life support in a federal penitentiary until you do.

Who knows what kind of hoops religion would make people jump through. Mormons will probably have to have a temple recommend before killing themselves.

Death with dignity isn't the answer to our dying woes. It's just another mental pitfall that people are willing to rush into. There are lots of alternatives to a tough life rather than killing yourself.

I'd personally be in favor of a constitutional amendment that allowed me to put someone else out of my misery.

G R A M P
CRAMP

Radio personality Dan Bammes is now a grandpa. I figured everyone should know because Dan is my friend and, frankly, I plan on ragging him about it a lot. If I turn up missing, please call the police and give them Dan's name.

My wife and I attended the party given in the baby's honor. Despite the infamous Bammes genes, the kid is actually cute. Looking at him Sunday night, I realized that it was only a matter of time before I become a grandpa myself.

While I'm no expert about grandkids, having them has to be way easier than having kids. In the first place, you know more. When my wife had our first kid, I didn't have clue one what to do. Not surprising considering that this is one of the great laws of the universe. If you want to find out just how stupid-to-the-bone you are, have a kid.

When the doctor handed me my first kid in '76, my initial reaction was that I was going to have to buy a bag of cedar shavings and install a pet door in our apartment. Fortunately, the kid also came with a mother, so it was OK.

Back then, I wasn't waiting for a kid. It just sort of happened. One day I was watching television when my wife suddenly turned mean and started to get big. A short time later, I was a father. As luck would have it, right before the deer hunt.

Prospective grandparents are different. They know exactly what's happening. Consequently, the waiting for a grandkid begins as soon as the kids say "I do." Provided that tradition is followed, the wait can last anywhere from nine months to, oh, say about 15 years.

Waiting for grandkids is accomplished in one of two ways. In the first case, the expectant grandparents don't make a show of it. They begin quietly stockpiling things for the grandkids: diapers, rattles, storybooks, etc.

I think I'm this kind of expectant grandparent. I already bought a baseball glove, a pair of football shoes (size 11), a video

game system, and a 12-gauge shotgun. I'm also building a swingset and a corral for a pony.

The other method of waiting is to back seat drive the blessed event. You see these grand-naggers hovering around the newly-weds as if the bride was a dispensing chute of a gum ball machine. It's non-stop, "When are you kids going to have a baby for us to hold? Have you been to the doctor? Are you trying to have kids?" until you want to kill them.

I wouldn't be so excited about grandkids if it wasn't for the fact that they're the best kind of kids to have. Done right, there's no bad side. They can be held or not. They can and should be fed the kinds of things you wouldn't have given your own kids. You just feed them sugar until they start to twitch like a clock tower sniper and then give them back from whence they came. It's called getting even.

Best of all, you aren't emotionally attached enough to grand-kids to feel obligated to get involved after they've done something in their pants that's bad enough to alarm the Environmental Protection Agency.

I'm betting that the thing a grandparent likes to hear most is "I love you." Conversely, the words grandparents probably like to say most are, "Here come your mom and dad."

Shoot, no wonder grandparents like grandkids. After raising real kids, they're a snap. They're the second most fun part of pro-creation. If you haven't figured out the most fun part yet, you probably won't ever have to worry about grandkids.

MATTRESS FACE

Ever notice how sleep actually makes you uglier? It's true. Every morning, I get out of bed, stagger into the bathroom, look at myself in the mirror and retch. While I'm no prize to begin with, I'm always forty times uglier than when I went to bed.

It might bother me more if I knew that this was a personal phenomenon rather than a human characteristic. But waking up ugly happens to everyone. In fact, a human being who just woke up is the ugliest thing on the face of the earth.

It's not true of animals. Birds always wake up looking the same as when they went to bed. So do elephants, penguins, alligators and panda bears. Scout, my dog, wakes up looking exactly like she always does—the product of an unnatural liaison between a pig and a really big hamster.

Scout is permanent press. When she wakes up, her eyes aren't red, her hair isn't something designed by an electrician and she doesn't have mattress lines running all over her face.

Me, I climb out of bed looking like I spent the night in a

ditch. No matter how refreshed I feel, looking at myself in the mirror is invariably risky business.

Waking up lovely is a lie propagated by television. You see this lie on the tube all the time: Man wakes up next to woman. They smooch, coo and snuggle. Man never wakes up next woman and runs away screaming. Neither do they give each other melanoma with morning breath.

When I got married, I thought I'd spend the rest of my life waking up next to a fairy princess. Twenty years later, I'm waking up next to—a fairy princess. And according to my wife, I'll continue waking up next to a fairy princess if I want to keep on waking up.

A survey in a women's magazine claimed that the majority of men said that women were their most attractive first thing in the morning. While this is absolutely false, it doesn't necessarily mean that the men were lying. They were probably just being true to their biological selves, which is really the only option men have.

See, morning just also happens to be the time when a man's testosterone is at its highest level. And being a man, I can tell you that when Mr. T is barreling through your veins, any carbon-based life form looks like Miss America.

Men are uglier than women when they wake up in the morning. That's because for men, sleeping is just another way of doing battle. Men move around when they sleep. The more you move, the greater the chance of sustaining mattress damage to your face and hair.

The average male sleeper covers 3.5 miles while he's asleep, making him slightly uglier than a sludge pond in July when he wakes up.

The effects of sleep ugly get worse as you get older. When I was a teenager, morning ugly was nothing that couldn't be fixed with a toothbrush and a shower. I'm 40+ now and it takes me three hours and about $20 worth of grooming products and medication before I'm fit to be seen.

Morning is also the time when it comes home to you the most that you're getting older. Every gray hair and every wrinkle on

my face was first noticed in the morning. I get up, peek at the mirror, and my first reaction is always, "Damn, that looks like my father but with leprosy and severe radiation poisoning."

Alas, sleep ugly is a terminal disease that grows until it kills you. The good news is that there's also the Resurrection or Reincarnation. And whether you come back with a perfect body or as a wart hog, you'll be better off.